Josh does an incredible job of directing hard-working achievers into authentic spaces that stimulate tangible goals aligned with the why in your life. Each chapter gives a call to action that empowers a person to high achievement through the analysis of our natural passions. Catalyst is a refreshing and practical read; one I'm certain that I will come back to again when I am in need of new perspective on reaching higher goals.

—John Chang, edupreneur, YEBW

We are all looking for the yellow brick road to follow in our careers, to have the courage and the drive to go where others do not. In his first writing venture Josh has chosen to pull back the curtain and show us all what it takes to be FEARLESS.

Knowing Josh is to see change lived out, a catalytic event happening in human form. He is a living example of someone who in this new venture to "put pen to paper" is a continuation of his life journey to be ALL that God has given him to be—a living catalyst.

—Keith Niccum, senior HR professional

Josh's transparency with his own personal journey and truth is incredibly impactful. His experiences and emotions are relatable, and moved me to reflect on my current state and trajectory, fears, and goals deeper than I have in the last 2 years. His recommended exercises are invaluable—spending time evaluating my own fears felt uncomfortable but necessary. Invest in yourself by taking your time with this book and work through each step with intention. Feeling refocused and reignited!

—*Megan Harrington, business development*

Josh McLean's Catalyst not only gives you the push to start on your next big project but outlines a framework to accomplish it. His positive attitude and personal stories motivate and inspire you to take the next step and begin taking hold of your future.

—*Euric Krause, finance professional*

CATALYST

IGNITE YOUR SPARK WITHIN TO ACHIEVE POWERFUL TRANSFORMATION

JOSH D. McLEAN

DEDICATION

Lisa: You are beautiful.
You are amazing.
You've kept me going on the darkest of days.
My gratitude is endless.

Bella & Hannah: It's impossible to imagine life
without your smiles and wonderful energy.
I'm so proud of you
and excited for your future.

YOU ARE MY LEGACY!

ACKNOWLEDGMENTS

As I reflect on my transformational journey, there are three groups of people who deserve my gratitude.

The first group is a small handful of people who believed in me and carved out meaningful blocks of time to invest in my growth:

> » Keith Niccum :: You showed me
> the power of mentors
> » Derek Glos :: You showed me
> the power of friendship
> » Dan Figurski :: You showed me
> the power of leadership

The second group is a larger host of people who shared in a portion of my transformation and have encouraged me to become a better version my myself over the years:

Lisa McLean, Nick J. Murphy, Kelly Killam, Euric Krause, Julia Kukar, Dave Goad, Gretchen Yeager, Amy Harmon, Shelby Scovel, Dylan Potter, Katie Nordstrom, Tom Wyatt, Sarah Redgrave, Gretchen Yeager, Josh Noda, Tony Amandi, Semira Sarancic, Steve Ballard, Megan Harrington, Jess Maki, Chris Oman, Jimmy Mott, Dee Philips, Brandon Reynolds, Ben Harris, Ian Strauss, Vernon Cropper, Adam Gooch, Doug Hannah, Stephen Mahaffey, Bill Terrill, Kristin Erickson, Rex Schneider

Reading personal development books was a major catalyst in my life. The third group is made up of virtual mentors deserving special recognition. Many people are producing new content every day; the message of these 30 people acted as a beacon of hope and helped shape my definition of an abundant life.

In no particular order:

» Brendon Burchard :: brendon.com
» Pat Flynn :: smartpassiveincome.com
» Tony Robbins :: tonyrobbins.com
» Tim Ferriss :: tim.blog
» Chris Guillebeau :: chrisguillebeau.com
» Stan Slap :: slapcompany.com
» Jason Fried :: basecamp.com/books/rework

- » Chris McKeown :: gregmckeown.com
- » Susan Cain :: quietrev.com
- » Dr. Caroline Leaf :: drleaf.com
- » Chandler Bolt :: self-publishingschool.com
- » Hal Elrod :: halelrod.com
- » Jeff Olson :: slightedge.org
- » Angela Duckworth :: angeladuckworth.com
- » Adam Grant :: adamgrant.net
- » Tom Rath :: tomrath.org
- » Tom Bilyeu :: impacttheory.com
- » Heath Brothers :: heathbrothers.com
- » Jen Sincero :: jensincero.com
- » Gary John Bishop :: garyjohnbishop.com
- » Simon Sinek :: startwithwhy.com
- » Shawn Achor :: shawnachor.com
- » UJ Ramdas & Alex Ikonn :: intelligentchange.com
- » Ryan Holiday :: ryanholiday.net
- » Seth Godin :: sethgodin.com
- » Josh Waitzkin :: joshwaitzkin.com
- » Dr. Carol Dweck :: mindsetonline.com
- » Michael Port :: stealtheshow.com
- » Judy Carter :: judycarter.com
- » Dave Ramsey :: www.daveramsey.com

TABLE OF CONTENTS

FOREWORD

Are you living your best life? Are you truly fulfilled with where you are in your relationships, career, health, and happiness? Or is the desire for more still burning deep within you, begging to get out?

What if I told you that creating a single spark can release the power within you and that, with guided practice and commitment, you can transform your life, shred your fears, and finally step proudly into your full potential?

If you dream of moving forward but feel stuck, unmotivated, cynical, or even downright pessimistic about your ability to make it happen, do not put this book down.

Catalyst is about creating personal breakthroughs and proving that, by igniting even the tiniest of sparks, you can transform your mind into a powerful flame, reducing your fears and insecurities to rubble. Once the tangled brush has been cleared, opportunities begin to sprout abundantly upon the ashes.

Catalyst teaches us how to unlearn our conditioned limitations, humbly embrace our insecurities and shows us how to turn our pain and regret into the fuel propelling us into a new season of life.

Josh McLean uses his powerful life story as an example of how he was able to overcome his deepest insecurities and fears to create a life on his terms. Josh's style is direct and encouraging. You will find his vulnerability is inspiring and authentic.

This book is tailor-made for the restless achiever—for the person struggling in mediocrity, hopelessly watching their flame dim over time.

Do not let that flame burn out.

You were put on this earth to serve a greater purpose. Picking up this book may well be the sign that you have been waiting for.

Your journey begins today. Prepare to ignite!

—Nick J. Murphy
coach, speaker, & best-selling author
www.nickmurphy.io

INTRODUCTION

Big Idea:: You were born for more, and you know it. The dreams and desires lingering inside you are achievable and exist to spur you to action. You are not permanently stuck in your present situation.

> *"People who live with huge, vivid, clearly*
> *articulated dreams are pulled along*
> *towards those dreams with such force,*
> *they become practically unstoppable."*
>
> —Jeff Olson
> author of *The Slight Edge*

Moving forward from your current situation requires vision, grit, and determination. How committed are you?

This book is written for all my fellow **restless achievers** out there! IF you are ready for change, THEN you will find tools to help create a meaningful transformation. IF you are ready to take action and explore achieving your full potential, THEN this book is for you. IF people around you think you are successful, but deep down you still have a burning desire inside to contribute more, THEN this book is for you.

What can you expect?

As you read this book, imagine looking over my shoulder getting a bird's-eye view of how I broke free from mediocrity, external fears, and internal demons. I'll share what worked well and what I wish I would have known sooner. These hard-won insights are what I hope to pass along to you, allowing you to potentially shave years off your own personal growth journey.

My objective is not to present a scenario where I'm better than you or have things completely figured out. I am still a work in progress. I wrote this book for those **looking for a strategy to gain new perspective and take ownership of their journey.** Through trial and error I have created an impactful goal-setting sequence that I am excited to share.

Most of the material we cover should sound familiar if you're pursuing personal development. Some information will be new, and other information will be sequenced in a way that you may not have considered. Regardless, I'm publishing this book because I believe the material will get you thinking in a new way about taking action to accelerate your dreams—action that changes the course of your life, creating "Aha!" moments along the way.

I have three desired outcomes for you as you read this book:

» A spark of hope and belief overcomes you and propels you into a new trajectory

» You take action on the tools and resources provided along the way, embracing a bias-for-action mindset

» A small seed of change is planted within you and harvests a transformational mindset shift over the coming months and years

Where do we start?

Imagine this as a one-on-one conversation. We could be meeting face-to-face at a Starbucks or passing time in an airport terminal. You have a few questions about the direction of your life and want fresh perspective.

My approach is mentor style; sometimes the conversation won't immediately make you feel warm and fuzzy all over. But certain things need to be said in order to nudge you and challenge you to take the next step toward your full potential. I'm not going to coddle you. I'm not going to tell you that everything's going to be okay if you don't take action. I *am* going to leave you with some actions to consider, but you own the decision on how you move forward with your life.

Throughout this book I agree to leverage my equation for personal strength:

STRENGTH =
AUTHENTICITY + VULNERABILITY + TRANSPARENCY

This formula is the foundation for everything I'm doing personally and professionally.

I believe change is possible. If you are reading this book, chances are you are ready to make some changes yourself. If you get started on this book and the material or tone doesn't resonate, I strongly urge you to put it down and find an author who moves you to action. Without action, you are learning interesting things but never moving forward.

Theory without application is useless.

What is your "Why"?

I'd love to hear your "Why." Tell me where you're at in your journey. What are you hoping to get out of reading this book? Why does this book resonate with you? What is your biggest struggle or obstacle you are hoping to overcome? Keep me posted as you navigate the steps contained within this book. Drop me a note on Facebook at www.bit.ly/JoshMcLean and tell me your "Why."

For this particular season, we are on a personal growth journey together. Let's strap on the seatbelt and see what happens.

Fair enough?

Who is Josh, anyway?

Whenever you are making the choice to consume information I believe it is critically important to understand the source of information and any underlying motives.

Based on this information, you should choose to accept it at a high degree of confidence, accept it with a lot of caveats, or laugh at the absurdity and walk away. That said, allow me to pivot and share my story.

My personal journey certainly falls into after-school special material. I navigated experiential learning, which is often the longest and most painful learning method. It could have been a lot shorter or smoother, had my experiences and challenges come in a different sequence. I'll give you snapshots of me at 10-year increments to give you a small glimpse into my winding path.

As of today, I'm married to my beautiful wife, and we have two amazing girls. I work at a small startup in Oregon you may have heard of . . . It's called Nike. We've had our fair share of medical challenges, but my wife has been able to stay at home to support our kiddos and focus on her creative pursuits.

That was not always the case.

Winding Road

Rewind the clock to Josh at age 5. Only child, born to a single mother in Eugene, Oregon. One of my first memories is throwing a temper tantrum at my own birthday party. Why? I have no idea. Not too long after that, I gained the distinction of getting kicked out of 1st grade. Montessori school, no less. Seriously, that's a thing; apparently you CAN get kicked out of 1st grade.

Fast forward to age 15. As a high school freshman, I was already on a first-name basis with drugs and alcohol. Basketball had been my identity entering high school, but bad knees accelerated my dropping basketball as a serious pursuit. I began to use drugs more frequently to fill the void of loneliness. My world took a drastic turn in 10th grade when I was challenged to attend college math courses at Portland State University. Having zero self-confidence and no formal support structure, I sprinted to substance abuse as a coping mechanism for fear. I allowed experiences at school to cement a mental script that I was worthless, that using my voice caused isolation. Drugs and alcohol quickly became my identity and contributed to an encounter with drug rehab.

Fast forward again to 25. With drugs and alcohol firmly planted as my identity, I raced toward my first rock-bottom moment by driving to work drunk one morning. This was a wake-up call. Very humiliating, very miserable, but ultimately a rock-bottom event leading me to a powerful "Aha!" moment. I found restoration through a relationship with God and motivation through a new job path which provided my first real encounter with personal development books. Those books provided the first flicker of a different world and greater possibilities. Around this time, I set off in pursuit of achieving my first 5-year goal-setting framework, a plan primarily focused on external goals built around what I thought success entailed. Along the way, I sacrificed my health and my relationships, ending back in a dark and lonely space.

Fast forward now to 35. Forced to bounce back from my second rock-bottom event. This time it wasn't drugs and alcohol but rather a car accident. I was rear-ended while at a complete stop. My diagnosis included a traumatic brain injury, muscle damage, and vision impairment. The road to recovery lasted over two years, and it was one of the most painful times in my life. The silver lining? I was forced to ditch my cardboard persona and external definitions of success. I had to dig deep and discover the true Josh.

"Human resources are like natural resources. They're often buried deep. You have to go looking for them. They're not just lying around on the surface. You have to create the circumstances where they show themselves."

—Sir Ken Robinson
education revolutionary & TED speaker

Where am I headed on the path to 45? Defining and navigating the pursuit of an abundant life is what fills my time. This is what I want for myself, what I want for my kids, what I want for you. Are you with me?

Stories like mine are everywhere. People such as Michael Jordan, Pat Flynn, Charlize Theron, Will Smith, and Sheryl Sandberg come to mind. I'm sure you have examples in your own personal circle.

Restless Achievers

It's likely you are reading this book because you find transformational stories inspirational and you are looking to make a change in your own life. If you are discontent with your current circumstances and know you are capable of more, you are officially a **restless achiever**.

Restless achievers fall into four main categories:

» *Continual Learner:* You are motivated by acquiring new skills, and you continually seek personal improvement opportunities. Despite this desire for achievement, you feel stuck in your current situation.

» *Dead Dreamer:* In the past you've dreamed of more, but you have temporarily given up on life. Your light has gone out, and each day goes by on autopilot without hope, joy, or excitement. If you stop long enough to think about it, you would say you are dying a slow death each day.

» *Externally Impacted:* A past event has put your life on tilt. You have might have lost a spouse or loved one unexpectedly, and now you are left without a true north. Internally you tell yourself you are too broken or overcome by the burden of obstacles.

» *Silently Fearful:* You have been playing small and never pursued that big idea you've dreamed about for the last 10 or 20 years. Internal fear, such as the fear of what other people would think, has held you back.

Each one of these situations requires a radical change to live an abundant life. It also requires awareness that your situation is not permanent, that *you can create catalyst moments in your life.*

Seasons

When discussing circumstances of life, I often use the phrase "seasons" to describe the ups and downs. When it's summer, you can predictably know when fall is coming. However, the timing of your life's seasons won't be predictable, but change is guaranteed.

Most people tend to overemphasize the permanence of today and hold onto present circumstances as a forever state. When things are really good, people tend to think life has plateaued and will be stable.

When things are bad, people lose hope and think good times will never come again. They fail to look back in the rear-view mirror and realize things change.

Certain seasons are a blessing and come with abundance. Others are tough, requiring you to dig deep to overcome hurt, pain, or struggles. Some seasons are short. Some seasons are long. Some seasons are hard. Some seasons are easy. Some seasons are dark, and some seasons are full of happiness. Seasons are ALWAYS in flux. You're always moving from one season to the next.

What season are you currently in?

I have not found ups and downs to follow a predictable pattern. It could be three years up and two years down. Your focus should be in this moment, right now, so you can be excited for where you're at today. If it's painful, that means you're growing stronger roots. If it's awesome and abundant, then be grateful. Don't overlook it. Don't forsake it. Most people ignore the awesomeness in their daily life and fail to appreciate the beauty and blessings.

Rules of Engagement

Let's wrap this chapter up by clarifying the rules of engagement. This is *your* journey. You are individually accountable for your own action. Your past is not your fault, but it is your responsibility to take ownership of your actions moving forward. That being said, if you have a situation requiring professional assistance, please don't be ashamed. Life can be hard and confusing, so get the help you need. Get it today.

What gives me energy is interacting with people motivated to make a change. I think of my role as an inspirational Sherpa: it's to highlight the best path for your individual situation. You are the one who must do the hard work of climbing the mountain to plant your victory flag. I'll be there alongside you to celebrate your growth and victories.

The ideal outcome is to have tight alignment of your actions to your goals. If you find yourself complaining about a situation, but you are not taking tangible action toward your goals, there is imbalance in your life. This requires honest internal dialogue. Either acknowledge the goal isn't that important or change your actions to get a different outcome.

Work in Progress

Personally, I'm still a work in progress. I'm not standing here in front of you to say my life is perfect and I have everything figured out. Now, me from 10 years ago? Different story entirely. I thought my contribution to society wasn't valuable unless I had reached a certain level of outward perfection. That was me playing small and living in fear.

I don't have all the answers, but I have been actively working on discovering my own path and doing the heavy lifting required to find my personal breakthrough moments. I can certainly speak from that point of view. I aim to be a positive voice in a dark space, shining light from my own journey and pointing you toward specific steps that worked for me. I believe these same steps can work for you. This is about creating momentum and finding progress.

On many days, I still find myself a walking contradiction. On one hand, I'm capable of extreme grit and determination when faced with chaos or crisis. On the other hand, I can be mentally weak and locked into a fixed mindset unexpectedly.

My daily habits, external actions, and internal mindset set the stage for subtle but powerful compound interest.

"Consistently repeated
daily actions + time = unconquerable results."

—Jeff Olson
author of *The Slight Edge*

How Long Will This Take?

Sometimes a leg of your journey is long. Sometimes it's going to be short. Other times you'll look back and to realize the most recent section of your journey could have been shorter.

That's perfectly okay.

Trust the process. Be grateful for your individual journey and believe in growth.

One of best illustrations I can think of is the journey of the Israelite people from Egypt to the region of Canaan. You may be familiar with the biblical story where they wander in the desert for 40 years before reaching their "Promised Land." To be honest, I had heard that story before but hadn't fully appreciated the personal application until recently.

Let's consider their journey in context of a map of the Middle East. It took them 40 years to enter the Promised Land. When you take out a map and look at the actual distance they traveled, you discover this 40-year journey could have been completed in six to nine months. Why so long? It took them 40 years because of their stubbornness and unbelief.

Wandering the desert was a consequence for many, but it was a personal journey of growth and strength for others. A journey that should have taken less than one year took them 40 years because of internal roadblocks.

Let's make sure your personal journey does not take 40 years.

Believe in yourself! Onward to the first step in creating your abundant life.

CATALYST

CREATE MARGIN

Big Idea::
Creating margin in
your life may be
one of the biggest
missing pieces in your
personal routine

"The ultimate value of life depends upon awareness and the power of contemplation rather than upon mere survival."

—Aristotle
Greek philosopher

Information Overload

Daily life for the average person is too noisy because they are in constant information intake mode, causing them to operate in perpetual information overload. Our brains are maxed out. This attention exhaustion creates unnecessary stress, both physically and emotionally. More subtly, it creates a disconnect between our stated goals and our daily actions.

Can we agree this is not a recipe for success?

Once you realize this fact and begin to listen to conversations around you, it's likely you will respond with either humor or frustration. You might find it somewhat comical as you hear people talk about how stressed they are, or how busy they are—when you just watched them "invest" 30 minutes in Facebook while sitting at their work desk. They're literally scrolling: consuming disconnected tidbits of information that aren't driving them forward.

This humor will turn to frustration as you hear the repeated pleas that they don't have enough time in the day. There is no room to do anything more, they argue—but you can see outside of their vortex, their information overload bubble, and clearly pinpoint how much wasted time is spent scrolling their life away. People generally want to have a positive perspective on themselves and achieve success, but often do not seek out their blind spots.

"In 2011, Americans took in five times as much information every day as they did in 1986—the equivalent of 174 newspapers. During our leisure time, not counting work, each of us processes 34 gigabytes or 100,000 words every day."

—Daniel J. Levitin
New York Times bestselling author

Overcoming information overload can be difficult because we are up against the smartest minds on the planet, who are intentionally waging psychological warfare on society to get our attention and keep eyeballs glued to the screen.

The only way for individuals to stand a fighting chance is to create the habit of temporary separation from external stimulus. Aim to become focused on a goal so compelling that the draw of information and constant updates loses its magnetism.

Have you ever considered why your best ideas come to you in the shower? *Whoa ... whoa! What are we talking about here? I thought the discussion was around personal growth. And now we've moved onto personal hygiene?*

Hang in there with me!

Whitespace Thinking

Whitespace thinking can be defined as a block of time set aside to intentionally reduce external noise and increase internal awareness. Think of it as a time where you can be with yourself with no distractions. Yup, just you and your thoughts.

This can be time spent internally focused in a reflective and contemplative state such as meditation. Or it can be a more active process and be time spent "deep-diving": get out a pen and paper and go deep into goal planning. It can be also active self-reflection where you give yourself some brutally honest feedback in order to identify and reconcile blind spots in your life. This could be answering reflective questions or focusing on a specific outcome such as goals for a 5-year plan. You may be doing a deep-dive session on how to launch your business or get a promotion at work.

Whitespace thinking is where the creative magic happens. This magic of maximum creativity and breakthrough occurs when your subconscious is triggered into action and alignment by giving your brain a space to ponder a particular problem or idea. This could be focusing on the problem directly or indirectly. This type of "margin" has become increasingly rare in our society due to the fact we live in a world where the average attention span is decreasing, while the average quantity of information consumed is increasing. We feel the need to be intaking information all day long to stay informed. This is the 21st-century version of keeping up with the Joneses. Fear of missing out (#FOMO).

I've seen the benefits of creating margin firsthand. This technique has been instrumental in my own life through taking new actions, thinking differently, and actively moving toward becoming a better version of myself.

The structure of your whitespace time might be different than mine—and that's perfectly okay. There are many books available focusing solely on setting up success routines, some looking specifically at the power of a simple morning routine.

"By simply changing the way you wake up in the morning, you can transform any area of your life, faster than you ever thought possible."

—Hal Elrod
speaker & author of *The Miracle Morning*

Whitespace Benefits

Many people jump in and start taking action without a concrete plan. This feels good because they are frantically in motion doing something. The problem is, they don't know if they're doing the right thing or if they're doing things in the right order. We've all been asked to work on a project or task and jump in without asking any questions. We immediately get to work, only to discover we answered the wrong questions. Pausing before committing to action creates an important buffer between thought and action.

There are two major benefits of pausing before action. First is the **power of no**. The biggest issue most successful people have is not necessarily stopping destructive habits. Rather, it's identifying choices or commitments that are good, but are not powerfully aligned to current goals. **Saying no becomes both liberating and empowering.**

The second benefit is **avoiding the action yo-yo effect**. Starting in a particular direction without considering priorities or competing demands means you get yanked back to a new direction in two or three weeks when a shiny new object comes into focus. This happens because you're not grounded on what is the long-term goal or roadmap. You are not clear on your definition of success. You expend tons of energy while never making real progress.

Chew the Clarity Cud

My next illustration might be a little gross—but hang with me. How does the brain process information and solutions to problems? Close your eyes and consider a cow chewing its cud. Gross . . . I warned you.

As a cow eats grass, it starts the first pass of chewing. Think of this as the first time you have an idea and you pause long enough to ponder it and consider its presence. Maybe it's a promotion at work. Maybe it's a business pursuit or hobby you've been considering for years. Or it could a be reflection, such as *what direction is my life going*? That initial pass is your first level of understanding. This is where you start "chewing" thoughts.

You chew it mentally and then kick it to your subconscious for mental digestion. That's when the power of your subconscious kicks in as it becomes aware of your intent to take action. It digests the situation and starts to bring all options into a new perspective and level of understanding. Then mental regurgitation occurs, and your subconscious kicks it back up to your conscious mind. Now you can consciously "chew" on this new information, creating a second level of understanding and awareness. Make sense?

This is where your subconscious starts to kick into high gear and gets excited. It interprets your serious intentions about taking action and further digests your thoughts. Your subconscious takes the second level of understanding you were chewing on, and it spits it back up to you, into your conscious mind, as a third level of understanding.

This phase is where information or perspective that you never considered together comes into focus and is connected in a way you could have never imagined. You sit back in amazement as mental light bulbs start going off. These deeper level insights are occurring because you allowed time for yourself to chew on the information, put it down, let it simmer, and then come back to contemplate next steps.

With this third level of understanding, you are now faced with a decision. Will you walk forward with faith and excitement in this new direction, or will you remain static?

It's easy to remain where you're at, to remain static, but trust me: a part of you will fade into the background and become transparent. Next time this same idea comes up, your subconscious is going to be skeptically hesitant and unsure if you are serious about taking action. **Fight the urge to remain static. Lean in and let go!**

Beauty in the Bottom

After my car accident, I frequently found myself lying on the floor looking for relief from pain. Being at home on short-term disability, all I had was time on my hands. More specifically, all I had was time on my *back*. I would be in so much pain daily I could often be found struggling to find the perfect spot to relieve pain. This gave me lots of thinking time.

I don't recommend this path for anyone. However, I've come to believe this car accident HAD to occur for me to stay calibrated toward my ultimate goal of living an abundant life. Serving a large corporate entity was a path to make a living and provide for my family, but it was not a path for me to fully express my superpowers. I needed a forced separation from the grind of day-to-day achievement to gain this clarity.

As I lay on my back, certain words would float into my head with vivid crispness. The overarching theme was "brain" and "mind." Initially, these were ignored because I interpreted the thoughts as lingering stress from my brain injury.

My interest in the mind and positive thoughts continued, but I did not explore them further at the time. I was at an emotional low point and ran a mental script on repeat saying the vision impairment from my injury meant I had to give up reading, my one hobby in life. My ability to read and stay focused without headaches was severely impacted. Unfortunately, I was stuck in a victim mindset instead of looking for what I could do.

Gradually, the seed of hope which had been planted in my heart and mind sprouted, and I was ready to take action. My interest in the brain and mindset eventually guided me to the science of neuroplasticity. This topic may be one of the greatest unlocks of the 21st century with relevance to all of humanity. Diving deep into this topic is out of scope for this book, but a quick definition may be helpful. Neuroplasticity, also known as brain plasticity and neural plasticity, is the ability of the brain to change throughout an individual's life-- e.g., brain activity associated with a given function can be transferred to a different location, the proportion of grey matter can change, and synapses may strengthen or weaken over time. If you are looking to probe deeper on the subject, Google is always your friend. I also have a section on mindset in my book club accelerator.

The idea of positive thoughts, a "growth mindset," or anything related to the subconscious felt uncomfortably New Age-ish when I first encountered them 15 years ago. Over the years I've encountered them with increasing frequency and finally had to recognize the mounting scientific evidence and anecdotes of successful people I listen to and follow. Creating a positive thought life is imperative to living an abundant life.

"Success leaves clues."

—Tony Robbins
life coach & motivator to millions

Commitment Required

So, what next? What do you do with this? My commitment is to provide practical tips at the end of every chapter. They will include tips and techniques I used to break free from the gravitational pull of mediocrity in my own life. They will also include tips I've gathered from others who have successfully created change in their lives.

To some, this might feel a little bit like homework—but are you willing to be proactive on your journey, to do the work required to reach your full potential?

Don't feel like you have to do everything I suggest. I'm attempting to download fifteen years' worth of a journey into a condensed list of things you can try today. Test some, try others, see if you get results. If something doesn't work for you, move on and find what *does* bring you to take action.

Create Momentum

What does it look like to leverage the power of whitespace thinking in your life? Here are my 4 go-to time slots when **intentionally creating whitespace thinking time.**

GET UP EARLY—DO IT!

Allow yourself a large block of thinking or creative time. I target a 60-90 minute block of time before getting ready for work. The focus can change each day, but I generally rotate through the following activities:

> » Work out with my wife
> » Meditate
> » Journal/gratitude
> » Read
> » Creative time toward large goal

(like writing a book!)

When you commit to getting up, make sure to set yourself up for success. Don't just set your alarm early one day and stumble into your morning; prepare your journey by making sure you think through all the steps. Preset the coffee, place your book by your favorite chair, set out a pad of paper and post-it notes if you are going to write. I also appreciate the power of music and will play Thelonious Monk or Branford Marsalis as background music because there are no vocals to distract my conscious thinking.

Keep your phone on airplane mode. Not "do not disturb," but airplane mode. Regardless of our best efforts, humanity is becoming more addicted to the mental distraction of our phones from continually checking them for updates. Think about it: how many times have you mindlessly grabbed your phone today? How many times since you started this chapter? How often to you check social media or email in the first 30 minutes of your day? Or right before going to bed? Set up the tools and resources to break the addiction.

DAILY COMMUTE

Tune into *yourself!* Keep the radio off for at least the first 20 minutes of your drive. (Tip: turn the radio off when you park the car at night.) I've found the insights from this commute quiet time to be as insightful as any idea that comes from the shower. Make sure you keep a small notepad in your car to capture any thoughts or insights before you step into work.

I often listen to an audiobook or a podcast during the second half of my drive. I'm not suggesting you never listen to music or talk radio; I'm suggesting you be conscious of investing in yourself first. People say they don't have time to learn or grow when, in reality, there is usually time in their day they haven't considered.

WEEKLY REFLECTION TIME

After considering the success habits of others, I've chosen Sunday nights for my personal reflection time. Keep a set time once a week, or every other week, where you slow down and look back to consider if you've been successful. If so, what has been working well? If not, what do you need to change in order to generate a different outcome? Keep in mind, this requires having a clear definition of success, your finish line. This requirement is where most people struggle. What time will you set aside?

HALF-DAY GETAWAYS

Schedule a morning or afternoon once a quarter where you can unplug from your typical day-to-day and carve out a large block of time to contemplate life in general. This can be at a local Starbucks or someplace more special, like the beach or a personally significant location.

Ask Good Questions

When you commit to carving out whitespace thinking time, it is critical to ensure you are asking the right questions. I've found two thought exercises particularly helpful.

START/STOP/DO MORE

This thought exercise is best done as part of your weekly reflection time and revolves around asking yourself three questions:

> » What do I need to start doing?
> » What do I need to stop doing?
> » What should I do more of?

The **start doing** list captures actions or habits you have been avoiding and you need to start doing. This could be starting a new information habit such as reading a personal development book for 10 minutes or listening to a podcast on entrepreneurship during your commute or breaks. It could be exercising or setting a weekly calendar reminder to call friends and family.

The **stop doing** list is just that—actions you need to stop doing immediately. Reflect back on destructive or wasteful habits that did not add value to your life over the past week. This could be things such as scrolling social media right before bed or checking email within an hour of waking up. It could be binge-watching Netflix every night while simultaneously complaining about not having the time or energy to get up early in the morning. What do you need to stop doing?

The **do more** list focuses on actions or habits you need to amplify. You might be mindful of your water consumption but need to increase the frequency in order to reach 80+ ounces daily. If you exercise occasionally, can you add an extra workout or two into your weekly routine? Maybe it's gratitude. You are occasionally thankful for blessings but find yourself stuck in grumbling mode on a typical day. By becoming intentionally grateful on a daily basis, you can help others around you switch their default mindset from grumbling to grateful.

What is on your list? This is a good chance to pause and take a few minutes to write down your initial answers.

80/20 Principle

Another powerful exercise to consider is documenting 80/20 situations in your life. I adopted this practice after encountering the book *The 80/20 Principle* by

Richard Koch and Tim Ferris's practical application in his book *The 4-Hour Workweek*. If you haven't read *The 80/20 Principle* yet, you should soon! It's a foundational element of the Catalyst Book Club Accelerator reading. (See www.catalystignite.com for details.) It was one of the original personal development books I encountered, and it was a catalyst to significantly change my perception of time and energy.

The 80/20 Principle asserts 20% of events in your life are causing 80% of your stress, pain, or frustration.

Conversely, 20% of events in your life are causing 80% of your joy, happiness, and satisfaction.

The first step in the 80/20 exercise is to grab a blank page of paper and brain dump a list of things currently causing you stress, anxiety, worry, or frustration. List out all the things, big or small, without any filters. Once all your sources of pain have been dislodged from your brain, then go back through the list with a critical eye. Begin to identify items that cause the *most stress*. Then narrow those items down to the *most painful*.

Eliminating or minimizing things from this list can often be the quickest wins to creating positive momentum in your life. Hold onto this list. It will be good material for an exercise later in the book.

The second step is to complete the same exercise for those things bringing you the *most joy and excitement*. What is the 20% that brings 80% of your joy? Maybe it's doing watercolor or drawing. Maybe it's playing board games with your kiddos. Maybe it's having a dance party with friends. Think about your last week, your last month; where did you have the most joy? What do you find yourself constantly dreaming about? What activities or projects gave you the most energy this week?

You now have a powerful summary of what is causing 80% of pain and joy in your life. This gives you a targeted list to explore as you begin to intentionally take steps of transformational change.

A final thought before you continue reading this book. Because this book is action-oriented, you may find yourself pausing mid-chapter to work through an exercise. This is perfectly okay! One strategy to consider is making a first pass of scanning the book so you are familiar with major ideas, sequence, and illustrations. As a second pass, come back to individual chapters and complete the "homework" or action items at the end of each chapter.

TAKING ACTION :: CREATE MARGIN

During this chapter we've talked about information overload, whitespace thinking, chewing the clarity cud, and asking good questions.

Here is a list of actions to get you moving toward creating margin in your life:

Commit to regular whitespace thinking time

- 20-30 minutes of morning "me time"; work your way up to 60+ minutes Expanded morning ideas can be found within The Miracle Morning: www.amazon.com/dp/0979019710

- Commute contemplation—keep radio off for at least half of your commute

- Set a regular weekly reflection block of time

- Schedule quarterly half-day personal retreat

Complete Start/Stop/Do More thought exercise

Identify the 80/20 in your life

- Brainstorm list of pain with no mental filters

- Review list and identify which items are causing the most pain (I'm a big fan of orange highlighters and yellow legal pad paper)

- Review highlighted items; separate into items where you have direct control and things outside of your influence

- For items outside of your direct control: can you minimize exposure or frequency?

- For items in your direct control: what can you do to eliminate exposure or frequency?

- REPEAT for list of things creating joy in your life

Practice gratitude: I enjoy the Five-Minute Journal.

- App Download :: apple.co/2NvOnxL

- Physical Journal :: www.bit.ly/5MinJ

Practice meditation: I enjoy the Headspace app (but many others exist)

- App Download :: www.bit.ly/HeadspaceForAll

Set phone to airplane mode

- Turn on mode 1-2 hours before bed

- Turn off mode 1 hour after waking up

BE STILL

IDENTIFY YOUR SUPERPOWERS

Big Idea::
You have superpowers!
Ignoring them creates
blind spots, causing
you to waste years
of life wandering
unnecessarily.

> *"We know from myths and fairy tales that there are many different powers in this world. One child is given a light saber, another a wizard's education. The trick is not to amass all the different kinds of power, but to use well the kind you've been granted."*
>
> —Susan Cain
> author of *Quiet;* superhero to introverts

Most self-help guidance focuses on the vision of "you can be more" and then triple jumps to "let's go set some goals." Setting goals is powerful and critical to achieving success. **However, the power of goals is magnified when sequenced correctly and connected to the idea of leveraging your personal superpowers.** Failing to consider goals in a holistic framework, or ignoring superpowers altogether, creates blind spots that will likely cause you to waste years of your life wandering unnecessarily, asking, "Where am I going?"

Your Superpowers

What are "superpowers" anyway? Superpowers are core elements of you that transcend any job, any situation, and describe who you are at your **highest point of contribution**. They are the essence of who you are, and they articulate your uniqueness.

At a basic level, these attributes generally present themselves during early childhood. These might be things such as how you organized your room or how you loved music and dance. They might be things such as drawing, communicating, or telling jokes.

Certain life events can also magnify and bring your superpowers to the surface. For example, when my oldest daughter was five years old, she came back from gathering candy loot on Halloween and quickly dumped the candy out on the kitchen countertop. She then began systematically organizing them into logical groupings— all the Snickers in one neat row, all M&Ms bags in their own straight row, so on and so forth. All of this without being told, without being instructed, without officially knowing anything about organization. She was only five years old! This level of organization and logic has become more magnified over the years.

My youngest daughter is energized by movement and music. You can usually find her bouncing on a ball or singing to herself. From a very young age, she has been very sensitive to the quality of fabric materials. Combine this with her creative side and you potentially have the next up-and-coming fashion designer. Her early work on creating fashion concepts has impressed me.

Many books have been written and many tests exist pertaining to the topics of self-discovery and finding your strengths. I personally lump these types of tests into two buckets: generalized and categorical.

Generalized assessments are tests like the Myers-Briggs Type Indicator®. They can be helpful since they provide a starting place for self-awareness. For instance, the MBTI® test buckets your personality into four classifications, expressed as a group of four letters.

Generalized assessments are good in the sense that they help create a macro overview and a common language to understand large groups of people. Unfortunately, they fail to holistically describe you as a complete individual. They don't capture your essence; they are capturing a reflection or a generalization about you. They provide a flashlight into general tendencies and potential job title matches, but they do not define your highest point of contribution.

I happen to fall into the INTJ classification which stands for Introverted, INtuitive, Thinking, Judging. I've found I don't share similar career paths or personal interests with many other INTJ's. The information is a good start but doesn't fully describe my essence.

Be warned. These assessments are viewed by the average college career guidance counselor as the primary self-discovery tool. Their advice is often tailored on defining yourself by a job title, with the implication your job title equals your identity.

If you take nothing else from this book, I plead with you to internalize this: **job titles do not equal your identity.** It's not just corporate workers who are impacted; college and professional athletes, high academic achievers, or even stay-at-home moms may be drawn toward this "identity theft" as well. If you generally attach your personal identity to your job title, you've been living a lie, and it's time to wake up. Maybe I'll focus on this topic in a future book and drill down on the idea that we have been mass-marketed this false concept which makes us impotent with regard to life's true purpose.

Alternatives to generalized assessments are **categorical assessments.** An example of a categorical profile is CliftonStrengths (formerly StrengthsFinder). I believe categorical assessments are more insightful since they provide a larger list of attributes. In some cases the attributes are condensed into larger categories to understand relationships between attributes. For example, the 34 strengths included in the CliftonStrengths assessments are grouped into 4 major domains, which were introduced in the Gallup company's book *Strength Based Leadership*: Strategic Thinking, Executing, Influencing, and Relationship Building.

Your individual profile highlights your top five strengths, telling you in which of the four domains they appear. My strengths are:

> » Activator (Influencing domain)
> » Achiever (Executing domain)
> » Intellection (Strategic Thinking domain)
> » Focus (Executing domain)
> » Strategic (Strategic Thinking domain)

You will notice my top strengths do not include the Relationship Building domain. This requires me to be more intentional as I navigate personal and professional situations.

Categorical assessments are valuable because they help pinpoint where your best work is accomplished and where the common ground is found between people with different strengths. So, if you don't share CliftonStrengths traits with a co-worker or spouse, you will likely share common leadership domains and thus understand how to communicate better on projects or tasks.

I hope we can agree that these expanded categories give you a more holistic and nuanced understanding of yourself. However, there are still some gaps to address which caused me confusion for many years. Without proper guidance, many people are left with the questions, "Now what? What do I do with these? What is the next step?" Uncoached or incorrectly utilized, it's like putting a Ferrari in the hands of a 16 year old without a driver's license. There's a lot of horsepower, lots of ground they could cover, but without direction or instruction there's greater potential for confusion, recklessness, or paralysis due to inaction.

The few who dig deep to stitch together both generalized and categorical assessments may still miss the core element of who they are. I know I did! Without realizing it, they look to external sources for validation. And—possibly more importantly—they miss the learning or the self-introspection from life experiences that have shaped them and their core beliefs into who they are today.

Coming Alive

My question to you is, what does a perfect day look like? What activities or pursuits make you feel alive? Where does time stop and you find yourself getting into the zone?

> *"In the end, mastery involves discovering the most resonant information and integrating it so deeply and fully it allows us to fly free."*
>
> —Josh Waitzkin
> chess prodigy & author of *The Art of Learning*

The clues are there if you start looking. Think back to a time when you came home from work and said,

"I had an awesome day!" Or you came home from a hobby event or you were at school and something happened in a class where you lost track of time. These are clues. Don't dismiss them, but don't overcomplicate them, either. Now might be a good time to grab your notebook so you can capture thoughts and ideas that come to you as you start the journey of finding your superpowers.

You might be asking yourself *just what, exactly, are superpowers?* I define superpowers as the intersection of personality and character traits describing you at your highest point of contribution. These are the core essence of things you are naturally wired to do, things you are good at, and things giving you energy.

A lot of times the answer, as you consider the possibilities, is right in front of your face. Often times it's not that you don't know who you are, you're just too afraid to claim your superpower and let go of false identities. We are going to face those fears together.

My wife, Lisa, is a great example of a childhood where clues were ignored and unnurtured. When she was younger, she loved art. She would draw and lose herself in a coloring book or drawing pad for hours and hours. She was energized by drawing, coloring, and scrapbooking. She also loved playing with hair or doing anything creative. Nobody encouraged her. Nobody helped her see this was a gift and talent. Not her parents. Not her teachers. Nobody acknowledged these passions to explore as career option.

As a result, she never considered the idea her love for drawing or coloring had a purpose beyond filling time once she left middle school; these passions faded to the background because it was time to get serious about life. She went to a community college in pursuit of an associate degree without clarity on what she wanted to be when she grew up.

Fast forward into adulthood, and the light bulb went off while designing our wedding and baby shower invitations. Clues were present before that moment, but an art challenge through an online design company called Minted was her personal catalyst for change.

Since then, she has embarked on a personal journey of self-discovery to become a self-taught graphic artist. She has profound appreciation for the amazing artist community at Minted, a platform where independent artists submit their artwork for feedback and approval by millions of online voters. It has been an amazing opportunity for her; she has won several awards along the way, as well as being featured in *Domino* magazine and in the Oh Joy marketplace, where they offer curated items by independent designers.

Looking back on life, many people say, "I wouldn't change anything." There's something to be said for the camp of *everything happens for a reason and a greater purpose*. However, Lisa's situation challenges that line of thinking; I'd even say we would change her story if we could. Who knows how much creative awesomeness she could have produced over the past 20+ years while her superpower lay dormant? I sometimes wonder about what path I would have taken if I had embraced my voice back in my youth.

However, everyone should pause and be grateful for where they are at in life, trusting that their individual journey has a purpose and is leading them toward their highest point of contribution. It seems **the straightest and easiest paths are <u>not</u> taken by the strongest and most impactful people**. What examples can you think of where someone has created great impact globally or locally that *didn't* encounter a hardship that shaped their path or perspective on life?

Frankenstein Expectations

Be aware of creating a cardboard persona from "Frankenstein expectations." Think of those life-size cardboard cutouts of celebrities or musicians. The idea of Frankenstein speaks to unnaturally stitching together your expectations of life and desired circumstances. Stop putting expectations on your life that don't fit your overall roadmap and personal definition of success. Social media doesn't have the answers. Stop looking externally to figure out if you are on track. Look inside; you have the answer.

Our objective in this chapter is to zoom out and identify words capturing you at your best. We tend to get confused when letting outside viewpoints and perceptions influence our answers before we independently reach a conclusion. Never, ever let someone else define who you are and what you are capable of.

Hear me out. Always consider the source of the information you are receiving. Most people are living in some type of fear, so why would you listen to them as if they magically have all the answers? Are you getting career advice from the perpetually unemployed? Dating advice from your single friend? They certainly have perspective and opinions, but not a tested roadmap or battle scars to prove that they've actively engaged in life and had to make personal sacrifices to achieve success.

Surround yourself with people who are pursuing similar goals or have portions of their life you want to emulate on your personal journey to achieving an abundant life.

Those images you see on Instagram, those videos or pictures on Facebook or pins from Pinterest about the perfect party, the perfect dinner, the perfect hair . . . They can be inspiring if used correctly, but often I see them become someone's expectation of what their life should be like 100% of the time. They fail to consider the fact that social media is a platform on which to put forth your highlight reel; it was never meant to represent all the messy parts of life. Celebrate the happiness others are experiencing, but don't let it bring shame or guilt for any difficulties you are currently experiencing.

Odds are, the real life behind the photo or video includes a healthy dose of pain and struggle.

My challenge across this entire chapter, this entire book, is to **DO YOU!** Period. Find the authentic expression of who you are. Own it. Live it out.

Do you have an idea on what this means for your life? Can you vividly picture what that looks like? Are you living in emotional or mental chains? What would happen if you were to break free from those chains and stop adopting people's expectations or circumstances as your goal? I think you'd be surprised at how many things you can let go of many things that will immediately increase your level of happiness.

"Don't let the noise of others' opinions drown out your own inner voice."

—Steve Jobs
Apple, Inc. co-founder

In the journey of finding my own personal superpowers, I've been challenged to ensure I'm asking the right questions. I recently had a chance to go away for a men's retreat that was labeled a "man camp." (I was jokingly scorned for using the word "retreat.") It was a chance for men to gather for three days of reflection and restoration. It was an amazing location in the Oregon desert. Did you know rainy Oregon had a desert right in the middle? This location also had the distinction of having no cell phone reception. The Wi-Fi was only for use by the employees. No cell phone calls, no Internet. Absentmindedly forgetting my bat signal and satellite phone at home, I had no method with which to interact with the outside world. What had I gotten myself into?

During these few days I had a chance to quiet my mind and turn off outside distractions. I took the opportunity to focus on what answers I needed to continue my pursuit of living an abundant life. For the past several years, I had been focused on asking questions like *how do I get a promotion at work?* and *what activities/pursuits should I consider to make more money?*

During this extended introspection at the retreat, I realized there was another question lingering beneath the surface that I had not asked myself since my car accident. I'm sure it's one you've asked yourself over the years.

What's my purpose?

Before this, I was focused on the next career move. Now, I was intentionally focusing both my conscious and subconscious mind toward achieving my highest potential. Once I was quiet, stepping back from the hustle and bustle of activity and to-do lists—creating margin in my life! —things started to come into focus.

On the last day, I climbed to the top of a large hill (what seemed like a mountain) at the cheerful hour of 4 a.m. Darkness was still upon the camp, and the air was crisp with a slight chill. Climbing this hill had been on my mind since I had arrived at "man camp," and I knew I would regret not seeing the sun rise from this vantage point. Embarking on this journey was something I had to do. Sleeplessness brought on by my overactive brain helped me get up before my official alarm; time to take action.

During my hike up the hillside, I was reflecting on the guest speakers and conversations during the entire weekend. I kept asking myself, "What's my purpose? What am I here for? What should I be doing?" I was stripping out all of the expectations, all of the pressures, and simply listening without rushing to solve the discomfort.

When I got to the hilltop, I was the only person there for about 30 minutes, until I was joined by a handful of other guys who had also decided to pursue a sunrise experience. As we sat in silence, we began to see the sun rise. My heart was in awe as I was taken aback by the beauty. All of a sudden I was hit with a peace never before experienced. Three statements were imprinted on my mind and heart:

> » "Serve others"
> » "Make others better"
> » "Your family is your legacy"

My next step was clear: making sure I live a life of service. Whether that's as a servant leader in the workplace, or helping others through volunteer opportunities, I needed to calibrate my time and commitments to ensure alignment to this vision. In the context of serving others, my service must also contribute to helping others discover a better version of themselves.

Your awakening moment doesn't have to come in dramatic fashion to be just as powerful. I'm not suggesting you quit your job and climb mountains until you find your purpose. My awakening moment came because I intentionally turned off external stimulus and tuned into my internal purpose. Once you turn down the noise in your life, clarity has opportunity to come, and your life can take on a different meaning. Implementing a weekly or quarterly reflection time will allow room for this type of insight.

Capture Your Essence

What's the takeaway? Make sure you're asking the right questions! Make sure that you're putting yourself out there and testing ideas. *Does this feel right? Does this give me energy?* The most consistent tool I've used over the past 10 years is my LinkedIn profile. Every three or four months I'll go through and read it with fresh perspective. From there I'll both tweak words and completely rewrite content, seeking a more refined expression of my superpowers.

With each revision I ask myself, "Does this truly capture the essence of who I am?" If it doesn't, that's a huge trigger to focus on revisions. As the years have progressed, my LinkedIn profile has come to capture a complete picture of who I am at my best, both inside and outside of work.

My superpower list includes the following attributes:

» Strategist
» Connector
» Catalyst
» Truth
» Clarity
» Humorist

WHAT ARE YOUR SUPERPOWERS?

TAKING ACTION :: IDENTIFY YOUR SUPERPOWERS

During this chapter we've talked about superpowers, Frankenstein expectations, coming alive, and capturing your essence.

Here is a list of actions to get you moving:

Additional resources:

- Simon Sinek "Why" TED talk
Website:: www.bit.ly/SinekFindWhy
- Myers-Briggs Type Indicator®
Website:: www.bit.ly/MyersBriggsTypes
- CliftonStrengths
Website :: www.bit.ly/YourCliftonStrengths
Book :: www.amazon.com/dp/159562015X
- *Bury My Heart at Conference Room B*::
Book :: www.amazon.com/dp/1591843243

Explore your response to the question, "Who am I?"

- Grab a blank piece of paper and jot down some thoughts. Initial responses typically include job title, family relationships, or responsibilities like volunteering
- External factors will never fully describe you, so dig deeper: what makes you tick? Think about what really inspires and excites you
- As you test each option, try to narrow your list to 5-6 attributes that fully describe you at your highest contribution

Ask yourself the following questions:

- What gives me energy?

- What hobbies or interests deeply resonate with me? Why?

- What do I get excited about when talking with other people?

- What activities cause me to lose track of time?

- Where does my mind like to go when I day-dream?

- What do I fear most?

- What would I regret not doing over the next few years?

Reach out to 10 or 15 close friends and colleagues. Ask them for short responses to the following questions:

- What do you feel are my greatest strengths?

- How would you describe me to other people?

- What do you enjoy most about our friendship or working relationship?

- What things might be holding me back?

P.S. You can find Lisa's Minted shop here::
www.bit.ly/LisaMinted

49

BE AWESOME

NEUTRALIZE YOUR KRYPTONITE

Big Idea::
Fear is a hidden
epidemic infecting
millions, silently
robbing people of
their full potential

"If you are distressed by anything external, the pain is not due to the thing itself, but to your estimate of it; and this you have the power to revoke at any moment."

—Marcus Aurelius
Roman emperor & Stoic philosopher

What are we talking about here? What is the opposite of a superpower? Kryptonite, of course. If you are not familiar with the Superman comic series, kryptonite is a green crystal-like substance emitting harmful radiation which robs Superman of his power. Too much exposure to kryptonite will kill Superman.

How is kryptonite linked to fear? As I quickly march toward my 40th birthday, I've been reflecting on my journey, mulling over recurring conversations with people regarding the search for meaning in life. As I contemplate what has held me back personally, and hearing from others in my sphere of influence, I firmly believe **fear is a hidden epidemic infecting millions** of people. Fear is a cousin of stress that has been increasingly linked to diseases and other negative impacts on people's life. Sure, "fear" is not a common diagnosis or a state of mind considered for treatment by the average medical practitioner. You likely won't find it during your self-diagnosis efforts on WebMD. Maybe someday.

Hidden Cause

Fear is invisible. Despite this reality, I believe fear is the origination for many present circumstances and perceived roadblocks. Fear is a force. Fear has energy. Fear cannot be eradicated; rather, it needs to be identified, neutralized, and put into quarantine. On some level, fear will always be present. **Ignoring fear magnifies its negative impact over time.** That's what made me associate "kryptonite" with fear. Living with untreated fear will silently kill you—and your dreams.

> *"Each of us must confront our own fears, must come face to face with them. How we handle our fears will determine where we go with the rest of our lives."*
>
> —Judy Blume
> children's book author

Fear does not discriminate against race, demo-graphic, or geography. Fear isn't a first-world problem or a third-world problem. As humans, we live in widely different daily circumstances and are shaped by differ-ent experiences. Fear is a powerful adversary and one of four worldwide commonalities.

We can agree there are not many common ele-ments shared by all of humanity. We don't all make equal money. We don't all start life from the same equal footing. We don't have the same family dynam-ics. What we *do* have in common is that we all share the same 24 hours in each day. We all need the basics of life, including food, air, water, and shelter. We all have a need for community—we were designed to live life through interacting with other people. The fourth element of commonality is fear.

Fear is a strong force impacting our ability to live fully and in relationship with others.

Fear Categories

Types of fear can be grouped into three main buckets:

» Fear of others :: What will friends, family, colleagues, or strangers think of me?
» Fear of self :: Internal fears about showing your true identity
» Fear of action :: Fear of the unknown, fear of change, or fear of making mistakes

Each of these global fears is manifested differently at an individual level. Some people might struggle with all three, and others might only wrestle with one. There is no right or wrong answer. From self-awareness comes perspective and the ability to make intentional steps towards change.

"Everyone has at least one big thing that stands in the way of their success; find yours and deal with it."

—Ray Dalio
hedge fund manager & author of *Principles*

You might not struggle with a fear of others, but you might be afraid of embracing your true identity. You might be paralyzed at the thought of making mistakes when committing to the next step of your goals. Fear of action may not hold you back, but you find yourself frozen when thinking about relational impacts on your family, or maybe even fear of rejection by your friends. Maybe it's insecurity about your appearance, a physical deformity, or a speech impediment. I don't know what it is, but as you go through this chapter I highly encourage you to keep your proverbial antenna up and scan for any undiagnosed fears in your life.

How Much Does Fear Weigh?

Fear is tricky because you cannot directly see it. You can't take fear and weigh it on a scale, but you can certainly feel it.

You can see it on somebody's face, you can see it in their eyes, you can sense their emotions. Fear can be quickly identified. You *know* when somebody walks into a room and has confidence. Or if they don't. HOW do you know? They are a human being, they have skin just like the next person, they probably haven't declared their lack of confidence out loud . . . but you KNOW! You can feel their fear and trepidation. Fear is a real presence in our lives. I plead with you not to ignore it.

"Constant paper cuts to the soul go unnoticed
and untreated, infecting our true sense of self."

—Stan Slap
author of *Bury My Heart At Conference Room B*

The power of fear might be compared to the power of wind. Can you touch wind or grab it by the collar? No, but you can feel it and observe the its impact all around you. You can't see it, but you KNOW it's there. You feel it hitting your face on a windy day at the beach. You can observe leaves rustling around on a brisk fall day. The presence of fear is observable in much the same way.

Once you learn to identify the presence of fear, you can begin to go on the offensive and neutralize its impact. Fear has a tremendously negative impact in your life and will be a constant companion who throws frequent accusations at you if you allow it. Fear makes you a fugitive on the run. Fear accuses you and makes you play defense instead of offense. Hear me on this: you are being falsely accused.

Our mission in this chapter is to go on the offensive, not to remove fear, but to neutralize it. Put it in quarantine. Once you neutralize it, you can harness the presence of fear to highlight areas where you are being held back from achieving your highest point of contribution. If handled correctly, fear can be used as a force for good.

Gainfully Employed

Fear has been gainfully employed in my life for over three decades. In my early years of exploring personal development, I was ignorant to the power of fear, and ignoring its presence in the pursuit of my goals created a framework for failure. Maybe not failure in the traditional sense, but failure to achieve my fullest potential, what I might describe as "neutered achievement." From an outside perspective, I made progress and even achieved challenging goals. Internally, however, I knew there was more power to harness. No amount of brute force or willpower or goal planning was able to overcome fear.

Advancing my life forward felt good on some level. I had become a better version of myself, but I was still not reaching my highest potential. Why? Our neighborhood bully, fear, convinced me to play small and do something a *little* better than before, but avoid jumping into the deep end of possibilities. I was afraid of putting myself out there. I didn't want people to see me for who I really was. Fear said I was not capable, not qualified, that I was an imposter.

I felt trapped inside my own body until I stood up to fear. Often, it felt as if I was being crushed by the hidden weight of fear, by an unwelcome house guest who constantly whispered to me that *nobody will like you for who you really are.*

> *"How willing are you to consider that your life is the way it is, not because of the weight of your circumstances or situation, but rather the weight of self-talk that pulls you down?"*
>
> —Gary John Bishop
> author of *Unfuc*k Yourself*

Paralyzing Fear

My own story revolves around being paralyzed by all three categories of fear. Fear of my own voice has been my longest companion. This fear burrowed into my soul around 7th grade, and over the subsequent decades it corroded my self-confidence, negated my contribution to society, and degraded any value of showing my true identity. It fostered an irrational fear of the judgment of others and a fear of making mistakes.

I've spent decades running from my voice—both literally and figuratively. Writing this book, I've begun to realize it's rather comical when considering the situation from an outsider's perspective. Over the course of these decades, the tangible fear of my voice has left a trail of pain, regret, and disappointment. But it's also had its glimpses of great power and impact when leveraged correctly.

For context, I'm a six-foot-three male with a fairly deep voice. I'm aware my presence can impact others and the environment around me. My wife frequently tells me to "stand up straighter"; she thinks I've been bending down to look smaller my whole life. When

I follow her advice, it feels like I'm a giraffe. When I stand up straight, speaking without mental roadblocks, I somehow feel like I've tapped into a greater power.

Growing up, Vernon was my one meaningful neighborhood friend due to the distance between home and school. (This might be a natural consequence of getting kicked out of 1st grade and being forced to find a new school on short notice.) With only three weeks of school remaining after my expulsion, major strings had to be pulled in order to avoid being held back a grade.

My first memory regarding my voice was at Vernon's house. We were coming back from playing basketball to grab lunch. As we entered his front door, the red notification light was blinking on the answering machine. *The what?* Yeah, I said answering machine. (For you Millennials reading this, do an image search for "answering machine" and get a laugh at the prehistoric technology.)

As he headed to the kitchen to make PB&J's, I stepped up to the answering machine and pressed play. Listening to the singular message, it was nothing earth-shattering. His parents were divorced, so it was simply his dad calling to check if he was around and asked for a callback. I dutifully went to the kitchen to let Vernon know his dad called. He turned his head slowly, with an eyebrow raised worthy of an Oscar, and said, "Seriously?" I replied, "Yeah, seriously." He said, "That was YOU, bro."

Please hold while my mind melts into a vortex of non-comprehension. "What do you mean that was me? That was your dad," I replied. Back-and-forth banter ensued as I remained confused on why he thought I sounded like his dad.

This would explain why my innocent phone calls to girls were received with distrust by heir parents. If I sounded like Vernon's dad, it was highly unlikely my classmates' fathers were buying the story that I was in the same class as their daughter.

I had become aware of the uniqueness and power of my voice, but I was still terrified and oddly ashamed. This weird relationship with my voice was further complicated due to family members having a hard time hearing me because of the pitch frequency of my voice. This created a strong connection in my subconscious that using my voice equaled isolation, which was compounded due to my geographical isolation from classmates.

It was a class speech in 7th grade that put my tailspin into high gear, providing the takeoff point of the fear I've been running from most of my life. What was this speech about, anyway? I recall having to give a speech in front of the class, but I don't recall the exact topic. What I do remember was my pair of black Air Jordan shoes. They were a little small because my feet had recently grown several sizes, and my left toe had begun to wear through the top. I still smirk when I think about using a black marker to cover up the white fabric showing through.

I recall standing in front of the class, frozen, barely mustering the energy to speak, saying, "Ahhh—ah . . . Ahhh . . . Ah." I don't recall the teacher jumping in to assist me or if I ever finished the speech. Over the past decades I've retained the emotion of standing in front of class, humiliated, scared, and terrified. As time went on, I became angry and I shut down. Did anybody notice? Did anybody care? That negative spark allowed my already low self-esteem to manifest into a raging inferno of negative self-talk, which, fast forward, created a perfect condition for suicidal thoughts and an overall negative mindset.

Off the Rails

During high school, my voice became a greater burden. I remember the desire to be silent in class to avoid getting humiliated. Don't join this club, because you'll have to talk in front of people. I found a way to tell one-liner jokes as a mode of creating connection while avoiding actual conversations. Larger social interactions were overwhelming and difficult to navigate. I was lucky enough to have a fully functioning body and mental capacity, so why was I so afraid to use it?

If you recall my brief life history from the Introduction, you'll remember that during 10th grade my life trajectory went seriously off the rails. I was naturally good at math and did not have to work very hard to understand the material. I used this mental freedom to become a profound distraction in class. One day, my math teacher pulled me aside and said I needed to consider taking classes at Portland State University. I was advancing beyond what he was teaching in class . . . and, yes, I had become too big of a distraction. I had no idea how to process going to a college campus when surviving the high school halls on a daily basis was difficult enough.

Remember my story about math in high school? With no mentor relationship or positive voice speaking into my life, I ran from the opportunity. Ran straight into drugs and alcohol as a coping mechanism. Eventually, those became my identity. Deep down, they were a masking agent for fear, for self-doubt. I put on a mask to hide the reality that internally I was scared. This false identify continued through college, and I stalled out, losing precious time in finding the true Josh.

I graduated college on time, but that small piece of paper did not provide me with clarity or direction in my life. Now, my mom—she never judged me. But I believe out of pity and not wanting to see her son fail, she pulled strings and set me up with an interview for a local grocery chain. Somehow I got the job and was accepted into their manager training program.

The comedic tragedy of my voice continued. My role as store manager in training required me to wear a red vest to identify I was the "PIC" or Person In Charge. Overall, the job entailed ensuring the store was running smoothly, that customer escalations were handled, and jumping into assist behind a register when necessary. Be friendly, be helpful, and make sure the trains ran on time.

Assumed into this role was the ability to use their overhead speaker system. Being frozen in fear, I failed this requirement and would literally run 10 aisles in order to find the person I was seeking. In hindsight, you could say I became "the running red jacket" in order to avoid impending humiliation. This personal struggle continued every day. Fitbit wasn't around then, but I'm sure I would have crushed my daily steps using this strategy of avoiding speaking.

Eventually I stumbled into a role with a financial services company. This was a challenge because I was forced to have sales conversations, but I did okay because the conversations with clients and prospects were conducted while sitting across a table. I enjoyed the aspect of helping people, and I was energized by solving the puzzle of helping others achieve their financial goals. Fear still tapped on my shoulder daily to remind me I was inadequate, telling me I was a fraud. I became the youngest district manager in the region, but I still felt like a fraud.

One of my biggest regrets was at the wedding of a high school friend. I went to his wedding and, I'm sorry to say, I failed to give a toast. I was so excited for him. He had been my best man, and there were so many things I could have shared from our friendship over the years. During the reception, somebody leaned over and asked me if I was going to give a toast. I froze. I was too terrified of what other people would think. I played small, looking down at my feet. That haunts me to this day. Not a story I've shared widely, as it still brings me regret and emotional pain.

Cardboard Facade

Embracing adversity after hitting rock bottom from my car accident forced me to let go of a brute-force approach to life and stop attempting to fit myself into a false mold. I had to lean in and let go. Despite uncertainty, this is when I started to figure out who I really was.

After my car accident, I took a new position, seeking a slower pace and more positive environment. During this transition, I could no longer expend the energy required to play "finance guy" at work. A short time into my new role, I was asked if I wanted to start traveling. This is something I had avoided in the past so I could uphold my personal commitment to be at the dinner table with my family each night, but I knew discovering my true identify would require getting outside my comfort zone.

The travel requirements turned out to be me giving short talks and training presentations. Fighting through the fear and doubt gave me unexpected opportunities, allowing me to embrace my true identity and uncover my unique style. Discovering humor as my core strength, along with a drive to create "Aha!" moments for others, made the exercise of speaking more of a stand-up comedy routine and less of a dry training presentation. (Maybe I should consider trademarking "The Funny Finance Guy.")

The next chapter for me, as I write this book, is embracing my voice and saying "yes" to something I've avoided for many years: joining Toastmasters. As of 2018, I'm officially a member, and I have opened the door of discovering the power of speaking.

WHAT IS YOUR KRYPTONITE?
WHAT ARE YOU RUNNING FROM?
WHAT ACTIONS CAN YOU TAKE TODAY TO KICK FEAR IN THE FACE?

TAKING ACTION :: NEUTRALIZE YOUR KRYPTONITE

During this chapter we've talked about fear as a hidden epidemic, the weight of fear, how fear paralyzes, and how fear creates separation.

Here is a list of actions to get you moving toward neutralizing your own kryptonite:

Watch Tim Ferris's TED talk on "fear-setting"

- Video :: www.bit.ly/TimFearSetting

- Complete fear-setting exercise :: www.catalystignite.com/resources

- Hold this insight for the Legacy Goals chapter

During your next whitespace thinking time, ask yourself the following reflection questions:

- What do I fear the most, personally and professionally?

- What am I running from?

- What visions do I repeatedly ignore?

- What are my biggest regrets?

- How many of these regrets are recurring?

BE COURAGEOUS

SET LEGACY GOALS

Big Idea::
Goal setting without proper guardrails can create unbalanced focus and cause unnecessary setbacks. Done correctly, goal setting can be one of your greatest assets.

"It's about being proactive about creating a life you love instead of meekly living the one you think you're stuck with. Give yourself the gift of a joyous life while you're still among the living."

—Jen Sincero
author of *You Are A Badass*

The average person does not actively practice the habit of setting goals. Of those who do set goals, most leverage the popular SMART framework. However, without a comprehensive framework, isolated SMART goals can create imbalance and potentially cause harm in the long run.

Done correctly, goal setting can be the most powerful tool in achieving personal greatness and advancing on your journey upward. Unfortunately, much goal setting is typically done too quickly, making the goals weak or ambiguous.

SMART Goals

The most commonly used approach for goal setting is SMART goals. It stands for:

S: Specific
M: Measurable
A: Attainable
R: Realistic/Relevant
T: Time-bound

For most people one of the biggest challenges in creating goals is making them specific and measurable. It requires the ability to narrowly define "success" and describe how you will know when your destination is reached. This crystallized definition of success should be compared against the typically vague declaration of "I want to make more money," or "I want to lose weight."

You must nail down specifics and set crisp goals. This moves the idea of "I want to make more money" to the specific goal statement of "I want to increase my base salary to $95,000 by January 15th." This statement has a clear definition of success—so clear, a random stranger off the street would be able to independently verify if you were successful in reaching your goal by taking a 15-second look at your pay stub on January 16th. Until you get this specific with your goals, there is ambiguity and you are at risk of dreaming, hoping, or hiding.

Blind Spots

The tendency for people is to get a gust of inspiration, haphazardly set an isolated SMART goal, and begin frantically running into action. This means people have started running in a direction without stopping to clarify the race of life they hope to finish. Where is the finish line?

After a few laps, the activity abruptly stops when they are distracted by another exciting direction they could be pursuing. This is the "yo-yo effect" of goal setting, creating an illusion of activity without any real progress being made.

"Don't mistake activity with achievement."

—John Wooden
legendary UCLA basketball coach

Other people cram too much into their short-term goals and end up getting overwhelmed. Think of somebody saying, "I want to lose weight", and then proceeding to attempt a transformation from couch potato to running five days a week overnight. This is admirable but not realistic. Nor is it setting the person up for victory. The first time they fail to run five days a week, this is viewed as failure. This perceived setback can perpetuate a mental script which says, "I'm a failure," or other forms of self-sabotage.

Goals should be considered in context of your overall personal and professional situation. Before any major actions are taken or commitments made, all goals should be explored. All options considered. From this list, a narrow set of goals can be selected, crystallized, and prioritized to ensure you are not sacrificing what matters most in life.

Exposure to SMART goals created the spark to complete my first 5-year goal setting exercise back in 2005. However, the goals I put on paper were selfish goals focused on external achievements, and they did not consider balancing life with my wife or considering my own health. As I looked forward to 2010, my

SMART goals contained a list of three achievements encompassing my definition of success:

» Obtain three designations after my name
» Earn six figures
» Work for Nike

What do you notice? They're all external validations, the optics of what people will think because of what I have achieved. These goals are not necessarily bad or evil, they were just not holistic. Focusing on these three goals meant I wasn't focused on my physical health. I wasn't prioritizing the relationship health of my new marriage. In my naivety, I assumed there were enough deposits in my emotional "bank," and I could spend three years pursuing goals with an opportunity to come back and fix any damage caused by my efforts to obtain those designations I was aiming for.

Fast forward. I completed my Master's of Business Administration (MBA) program with near-perfect grades and passed the three CFA® (Chartered Financial Analyst) exams simultaneously, which is a rare occurrence. On paper, I was successful; I could check off the first of my three goals, since I had achieved another designation before starting the MBA/CFA route. In reality, the results were mixed because I had gained almost 40 pounds, and my marriage was intact only because of the determination and faith of my wife!

Legacy Questions

Earlier in the chapter I outlined how my initial attempts at goal setting were externally focused. I prioritized academic achievement to the exclusion of my body and soul. How did I get started down that path? I started with "how do I stop being a failure?" which led me to "what does success look like?" Not inherently bad questions, but the next question is where things went awry. "What accomplishments will make me feel I'm successful when others look at me?"

This thinking forced me to adopt other people's measures of success. I looked to friends who were making more money. I looked to people on LinkedIn I thought were successful and noticed they had letters after their names. I looked to articles talking about a successful salary. Flawed logic.

The questions I should have been focused on, and the ones I want you to start asking, are ones like these:

- » What gives me energy?
- » Who do I want to be in the short-term?
- » Who do I want to be in the long-term?
- » What type of impact will I have?
- » What kind of spouse or parent do I want to be?
- » What do I want to be known for when I'm 30, when I'm 50, when I'm 70?
- » What will I regret not doing?
- » When I pass away what will be my legacy?
- » What will people celebrate at my eulogy?

Legacy Goal Overview

Legacy Goals are my antidote to lopsided SMART goal setting, the next generation of goal setting building upon the framework of SMART goals. Think of it as SMART goals packaged within a framework of vision, passion, and holistic alignment.

The outcome is a tool allowing you to tightly align actions taken today to your long-term goals without making unnecessary sacrifices. This creates a repeatable process to help accelerate the journey of achieving your full potential. Done correctly, this produces a balance of mind, body, and soul. Moving from SMART goals to Legacy Goals is what helped me reset my trajectory and find a healthy balance in all aspects of my life.

At the highest level, you can conceptualize Legacy Goals as having two dimensions: Time and Legacy Categories. The horizontal axis represents time. And the vertical axis represents the most important categories in your life.

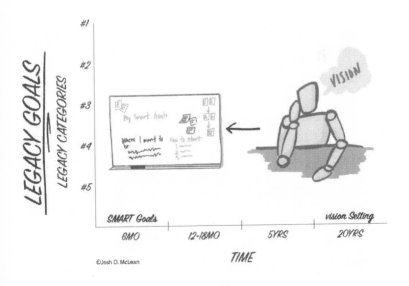

©Josh D. McLean

The Time dimension is broken up into four time horizons:

> » 6 months: looking at life and opportunity right in front of you
> » 12-18 months: just beyond the horizon but close enough to get specific
> » 5 years: what success looks like in the medium term driven by powerful "why"
> » 20 years: long-term vision of your abundant life

The Legacy Category dimension represents the most important areas in your life that need focused attention over a 20-year horizon. These might represent things you want to be remembered for at your eulogy, such as these:

> » Marriage
> » Parenting
> » Health
> » Career
> » Hobbies/pursuits
> » Relationships
> » Mentoring

I believe well-rounded Legacy Categories include serving others in some aspect. Your greater reason and purpose for living is often found outside of yourself as you give back to others.

> *"If you're not making someone else's life better, then you are wasting your time. Your life will become better by making other lives better."*
>
> —Will Smith
> actor & film director

Legacy Goal Setting

Here are the steps to create powerful Legacy Goals.

ACTIVITY #1: BRAINSTORM CATEGORIES

Your objective in Activity 1 is to brainstorm all possible Legacy Category ideas that come to mind. From there, you need to review the possibilities and narrow the list to six to eight categories having the most personal meaning over a 20-year period. This might mean grouping several related ideas into a larger umbrella category. There are general categories to consider, but ultimately these categories must resonate deeply with you and inspire you. They represent your personal definition of an abundant life.

Once you have your preliminary Legacy Categories defined, you will work right to left.

ACTIVITY #2: BRAINSTORM 20-YEAR VISION

Your objective in Activity 2 is to describe your vision of success for each of the categories you defined in activity 1. What is the most compelling future vision that makes you smile and gives you extreme happiness? There is no standard "right" answer. You can't look over someone else's shoulder for the answer. This is YOUR future! Close your eyes and imagine what success looks like. Your aim here should be a single-sentence vision statement for each category.

ACTIVITY #3: BRAINSTORM 5-YEAR VISION

Your objective in Activity 3 is to consider what would have to be true in 5 years for you to be on track to accomplish your 20-year vision statement.

For example, if paying for a portion of college expenses is part of your "financial" Legacy Category, how much money would you need to save in the next 5 years? If traveling internationally once a year is part of your "adventure" Legacy Goals, how much money will you need to set aside? The list of goals in this time horizon should generally feel like stretch goals that are a mix of scary and exciting to consider.

ACTIVITY #4: BRAINSTORM SMART GOALS

Your objective in Activity 4 is to break down what would have to be true in 12-18 months for your 5-year vision to be on track. Repeat for a 6-month time horizon. Statements in these two time periods should be SMART goals. (You will likely have 2 or 3 SMART goals for each time horizon category.)

ACTIVITY #5: CALIBRATION

Up until now you've been considering each category in isolation. Now you need to review the list of goals across each time horizon and consider the sheer volume of goals. You must seriously consider how time spent pursuing one category reduces your available free time and might require a tradeoff in another category.

Activity 5 might require a few passes as you consider what you really want to achieve versus what level of commitment you can actually make. To pursue your goals with passion and excellence, it's likely something must sit on the sidelines. What remains are the categories and goals which require an intentional investment of time and energy to nurture and grow over the long term. For example, I've made the decision to not pursue golf because I'm investing time in my marriage and kids. I still find the idea of golf appealing and might take it up down the road. For now, I can confidently say it's not a legacy priority.

ACTIVITY #6: DEFINE ACTIONS

With your 6-month SMART goals defined, you now can create an immediate action list. What actions would you need to take in the next two weeks to create momentum toward your 6-month goals? You can think of these as your list of 80/20 Actions.

Some of you might be feeling slightly overwhelmed. Before you get too frustrated, **I'll remind you the process is iterative**—you'll have the chance to revisit the process later.

This process should also be exciting. These are your most important goals defining ultimate success for your life!

Chew the clarity cud on this one. Write your initial answers down for these questions, then walk away for a few days, giving your subconscious time to activate and get you to the next level of understanding.

> *"Our goals can only be reached through a vehicle of a plan, in which we must fervently believe, and upon which we must vigorously act. There is no other route to success."*
>
> —Pablo Picasso
> Spanish painter & Cubanism pioneer

Check Your Vision

If you start to focus your mind around defining your legacy and pour your energy into exploring your individual answers, everything will *slowly* come into focus.

At first, your understanding and vision will be fuzzy. This is okay. Think of your annual visit to the eye doctor. During your eye exam, the optometrist sits you down in a chair and displays a few fuzzy images on the wall, then proceeds to repeatedly ask you which one is clearer, option one or option two. You think they are both imperfect, but option one is better. This continues back and forth for a few minutes as things slowly come into focus. You may want to jump to the final answer, but **the process of discovery provides important information** for the doctor. The same is true for the process of defining your Legacy Categories.

As you narrow down your Legacy Goals you will be revisiting several questions until you achieve 20/20 vision:

» Is this list complete? (Does it represent everything I desire to accomplish?)

» Do the items on my list give me energy?

» Is there anything missing from the list I would regret not pursuing?

» Can I carve out reasonable blocks of time each week to pursue these goals with excellence?

To gain clarity you will need to repeat this process so your subconscious can unlock new levels of understanding. That is the heavy lifting. There is no "easy button" on this exercise. You must commit to climbing the mountain and have the mental and emotional strength to reach the top. You will have to deal with uncertainty and messy thoughts as you navigate iterations.

I don't regret setting my original goals back in 2005, since they were a stretch for my circumstances at the time. I had an average college GPA. I was barely making $30,000 a year and felt lucky to be employed. To say I wanted to work for a global brand icon and earn 4 times my current income was a huge mountain. I wanted to provide a greater life for my family. Looking back, I wish I had a more complete definition of success and a better roadmap to find true success and happiness. This order of this book was intentionally sequenced to strengthen your goal-setting competency and accelerate your self-realization to help you identify what is truly important to you.

"Maturity is the ability to reject good alternatives in order to pursue even better ones."

—Ray Dalio
hedge fund manager & author of *Principles*

"No" and "Not Now"

As you start to refine your Legacy Goals, you will encounter a phase where prioritization gets difficult and you may want to walk away. Hang in there with me. Once people start the brainstorming process they tend to get excited about the possibility of achieving all the goals and dreams that have been in their head. Then they may get a little discouraged when the realize they don't have time to accomplish ten new things this year.

Finishing Legacy Goals requires you to take lower-ranking goals, say "not now," and push them out to the future. Or say "no" and have the courage to acknowledge this particular goal is interesting, but ultimately it conflicts with larger and more important priorities. **Saying "no" or "not now" is one of the most powerful tools to harness your energy and focus.**

> *"Use the power of no to get your priorities straight. You rarely regret saying no. But you often wind up regretting saying yes."*
>
> —Jason Fried
> co-founder of 37Signals

Why are these phrases so powerful? Why is saying "no" or "not now" often more powerful than saying "yes"? It forces you to focus, to align your actions to prioritized commitments. You weed out the good possibilities you *could* do in favor of the great accomplishments you *MUST* do! Most personal power diminishes due to overextending yourself or trying to master too many new things at once. You must properly sequence new commitments to avoid reaching burnout.

TAKING ACTION :: SETTING LEGACY GOALS

This chapter has one big action item:

Set your Legacy Goals:

> » Activity #1 :: Brainstorm your
> Legacy Categories

> » Activity #2 :: Brainstorm 20-year
> vision for each category

> » Activity #3 :: Brainstorm 5-year
> vision for each category

> » Activity #4 :: Brainstorm SMART
> goals for 6-month and 12- to
> 18-month time horizons

> » Activity #5 :: Calibration to ensure goals
> are realistic when considered holistically

> » Activity #6 :: Define actions you can take
> today aligned to 6-month SMART goals

Grab my Legacy Goals Excel template:
www.catalystignite.com/resources

BE BOLD

CREATE SUCCESS SPARKS

Big Idea::
Your current state is
not permanent.
The Power of Now
creates Success Sparks.
A small spark can create
impact lasting decades.

*"A real decision is measured by the fact
that you've taken a new action. If there's
no action, you haven't truly decided."*

—Tony Robbins
life coach & motivator to millions

Congratulations! You are nearing the finish line. Once your destination is identified, it's now time to invest energy in creating momentum. This is the fun part, where you start to complete the 80/20 Actions you identified in Activity 6 back in Chapter 4. These are the near term actions aligned to each of your Legacy Categories. Don't overcomplicate the process; these are the absolute next steps to take to achieve your abundant life. Narrowing down actions to this level exponentially accelerates the odds of finding inspiration and getting into the zone.

A **Success Spark** is a small positive spark of action. These sparks can change your trajectory for a decade, or even more. It's important to focus on creating the correct type of sparks, because the trajectory created can be positive or negative.

Before we go any further, I'm sure you've already come to this realization but it's worth repeating: **your current state is not permanent.**

Did you hear me?

> *[Megaphone voice] Your current*
> *state is not permanent!*

Life circumstances are constantly changing and evolving. Even if things are going well, that is not a guarantee for future performance. I'm betting you understand this reality but fail to apply to your own life circumstances.

You Happen

You may have been headed in one direction with a perfect plan when, all of a sudden, your path changed and now you have to figure out what to do next. That's okay; that's not a bad thing. That's how a lot of us have experienced life. You may have had an external event occur that was out of your control. For me, it was a car accident; for others, it's been the loss of a loved one. Or possibly it's been a recent job restructure in corporate America leaving your retirement uncertain. Or you could just be starting out and not quite sure what to do with your life.

My challenge for you in this chapter is to consider the fact that **sometimes YOU happen**. You have the ability to harness energy from external circumstances to create a spark of change and build momentum toward the life you want to live. Things can happen to you, or you can choose to make things happen.

"An object either remains at rest or continues to move at a constant velocity, unless acted upon by an external force."

—Sir Isaac Newton
physicist & inventor of Newton's Law of Motion

At the end of the day, everyone reaches a destination. My question to you is, will it be the destination that you want to reach?

Last chapter we identified Legacy Goals that are your personal roadmap—your true north, so to speak—to keep you motivated during the daily grind of advancing your goals. One step in front of the other isn't generally sexy to talk about, but it's the only way to reach any meaningful destination. There are no express trains. Some people focus on buying a winning lottery ticket but, statistically speaking, those people are going to be broke within a few years. If you find yourself in a fixed mindset hoping for leprechauns to show up at your doorstep with pots of gold . . . then we might need to have a different conversation.

The Power of Now

The power of now is focused around taking actions in the moment. Not about *thinking* of taking action, but actually *taking action*. Actually getting out there and doing something. It's about stoking the fire and building excitement in your life.

One of the biggest drivers toward taking more action in my own life was *slowing down*. Carving out dedicated quiet time somehow triggered my mind to move from reactive to proactive. **This is the power of whitespace thinking in action**. Once I quieted both the external and internal noise, I began to feel these powerful prompts coming forward clearly.

Moving from vision to taking immediate action is the **power of now.** To-do lists have become an important part of surviving in society, but I don't believe we were created only to check boxes on to-do lists. Having the confidence to briefly let go of your list and be present in the moment creates powerful internal alignment. I regularly set goals for each day but am always primed and ready to take action should I be given a chance to practice the power of now. This keeps me connected me to my greater purpose and my greater calling.

Taking action should be a mix of planned actions aligned to your 6-month goals along with promptings and inspiration coming to you throughout the day. These inspirations could be dismissed as distractions but often this is your subconscious aligning to your goals and prompting you to powerful actions in the moment.

What does this look like practically? I carry around a folded 8.5"x11" piece of paper with my 6-month goals distilled down to "MUST accomplish actions" over the next two weeks. I refer to these as my 80/20 Actions. Scanning this list and repeating personal affirmations is part of my daily routine. This practice helps me stay grounded amidst the chaos and fluidity of the day as new possibilities arrive at a constant pace.

Having confidence and clarity from Legacy Goals allows me to quickly assess whether new actions and opportunities are potentially aligned to my long-term goals. Is this new shiny object really an important goal? Most often this shiny object is interesting because I'm procrastinating 80/20 Actions. Deep down, I'm self-sabotaging or scared to do the work that I know I need to get done.

Newton's First Law of Motion

In order to change our current trajectory, we need to inject new energy and new action to create different outcomes. **Everyone needs a catalyst**. We need some type of energy or force to impact us. Most people contemplate this idea and associate the prospects of change as positive. It's important to understand that sometimes sparks can be negative. It might be something that you *didn't* do, thus creating a negative spark and a negative mindset. It could be an external event triggering a negative trajectory. There have been several major forces in my life creating a change in trajectory.

In seventh grade, my speech failure was a negative trajectory, creating three decades of impact. Countering with positive sparks in the area of my voice has been a mix of fun and scary. New sparks have come from creating situations where I'm around motivated individuals, helping them create their own "Aha!" moments. Joining Toastmasters has been another positive spark.

Sparks are inherently small. Often you don't know which spark is going to ignite action. If you've ever tried to light a campfire, think of how many sparks it took to get the fire going. Creating success sparks in your life is the same way. **Have faith that small actions will result in powerful outcomes.** My daily whitespace time is my favorite time to get clarity on what small actions I can take to spark new momentum.

The Power of Mentors

Beyond books, mentor relationships have had the most transformational impact in my life. The economy wasn't great coming off my MBA and CFA® Program completion, and I felt stalled out on next steps. My internal drive was intact, but I felt rudderless.

During this period, I became acutely aware of my lack of self-confidence. I became a bit frustrated and grumpy during this season. Thankfully, I connected with someone who opened my mind up to a whole new universe of thinking and possibility. Keith became my mentor, and his impact has been a game-changer. His influence is part of the reason I'm driven to give back and help others reach their own breakthrough "Aha!" moments.

Mentor Impact Model

Over the years, I've wrestled with why it took me so long to get to a spot of positive change. While I had a few people in my life quietly supporting me, I had nobody taking an active vocal interest or spending time and sharing wisdom to help me understand life.

I created the Mentor Impact Model to capture my observations and beliefs about influence. This framework helped crystallize why prior family or school interactions failed to facilitate a catalyst for change.

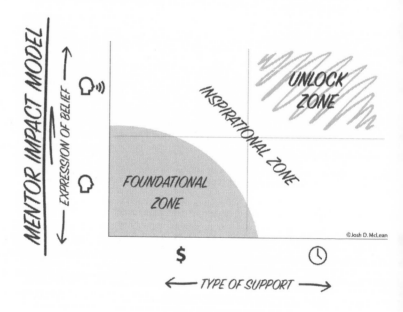

The impact of mentorship can be understood by considering two variables. First is the **type of support**. Second is the **expression of belief**.

On the horizontal axis is type of support, which is split between financial assistance and investment of time. On the vertical axis is expression of support, which is split between silent supporter and vocal supporter.

In the bottom left quadrant reflects **foundational support**. The type of "love" I got in my family was in this quadrant. In the nonprofit world, these would be financial donors.

Looking back, I can understand why this type of support was the most likely path for my mom. Every day she went to work in an environment where she was literally told, "Women don't belong in the workplace." This type of harassment is more stressful than most people could handle on a daily basis. She exhibited great determination and resolve to stay focused on supporting the family. But that didn't leave a lot of time to invest in 1-on-1 interactions. Her stress release in the evening of yelling on the phone made it easier for me to fade into the background and stay busy playing video games.

I'm thankful for her quiet support and determination which created an environment where I observed grit on a daily basis. This has stuck with me throughout my professional career.

On the opposite end of the spectrum from foundational support is what I call the **unlock quadrant.** This is the top right quadrant, reflecting vocal support enhanced by an investment of time. This zone reflects my 1-on-1 interactions with my mentor.

His level of financial investment was minimal, about $3-4 for an occasional cup of coffee, but his level of time commitment was huge. He regularly carved out space from his day to meet with me and provided the most precious resource, his time. He pressed pause on his day and wasn't distracted by his phone or conversations going on around us. This was somewhat unfamiliar because nobody had really invested time in me growing up. I was around other people but always felt nobody would care or notice if I disappeared.

"Show me a successful individual and I'll show you someone who had real positive influences in his or her life. I don't care what you do for a living—if you do it well I'm sure there was someone cheering you on or showing you the way. A mentor."

—Denzel Washington
actor & film director

The other big change coming from my mentor relationship was the type of belief Keith demonstrated. He gave me vocal, active encouragement. This wasn't piffy Facebook motivational candy, but rather a deep belief in my potential along with an **ability to compassionately challenge the beliefs holding me back**, keeping me imprisoned in status quo.

Wait a minute . . . just wait a minute . . . I can hear you saying. *Didn't that math teacher you mentioned earlier provide vocal support?* Yes, he was vocal, but he did not provide the support structure of time to help me bridge the gap of my current state to his vision of my potential. Without someone to walk alongside me, fear took over and I gravitated toward destructive behaviors.

My challenge to you is to consider how you are showing up in other people's lives. You could be the equivalent of my 10th-grade math teacher, having good intentions but ultimately being a drive-by mentor. If you are not willing to pause and invest your time—or connect them with meaningful resources to help bridge a gap—**you could be setting them up for more harm than good.**

TAKING ACTION :: CREATE ACTION SPARKS

During this chapter, we've talked about the power of now and creating momentum by intentionally creating action sparks. We've covered the Mentor Impact Model and the different levels of support you can give someone when seeking to make an impact.

Here is a list of ideas to get you moving toward creating action sparks:

Create future momentum

Purchase *The Slight Edge* by Jeff Olson today. Feel free to jump over to Amazon and buy it right now. (I'll wait.)

The ideas contained within *The Slight Edge* are so powerful I've put this as the first book on my Catalyst Book Club Accelerator reading list.

Book :: www.amazon.com/dp/1626340463
Access more accelerator resources ::
www.catalystignite.com/resources

Take action

Make progress on 80/20 Actions aligned to your Legacy Goals from the last chapter. You've started those, right? Grab several blank pieces of paper and drill down on next steps for each of your 6-month horizon goals.

Questions to ask yourself:

» What needs to happen in 3 months to accomplish my 6-month goals?

» What needs to happen in the coming month to be on track for my 3-month goals?

» Break it down further until you have a list of next steps for a 2-week period. **This becomes the list of actions you MUST accomplish—your 80/20 Actions.**

Clarity on these actions puts you in a position where you will be pursuing smaller, more achievable goals and creating momentum. This momentum will allow you to crush your 6-month goals. Also, when narrowing your focus to a 2-week time horizon, you don't have to carry the burden around of completing your longer-term horizon goals.

The longer-term vision remains the inspiration, giving you energy, but you aren't getting stressed on the "how" just yet. You'll sleep well at night, having the confidence that you're committed to doing the required activity you've laid out over the next two weeks.

Expand your horizon

Identify 10 people in your local area to reach out and request a 15-minute conversation over coffee.

Look for people you find inspiring or who have influenced you. Who is in your vicinity that is currently living some element of your ideal life? The type of people on this list will vary greatly from person to person.

I understand this might be outside of your comfort zone—but **you never know what is on the other side of fear**. Through these conversations you'll meet some fun people and likely make some unexpected connections. You can also expand this out to be Skype or FaceTime calls.

BE EXPECTANT

FEEDBACK LOOP

Big Idea::
After formal schooling
we are thrust into an
unstructured abyss of
decisions, forced to fend
for ourselves. You own
creating your personal
syllabus of success.

"Feedback is the breakfast of champions."

—Ken Blanchard
author & thought leader

We have officially entered maintenance mode, where the rubber meets the road. Here, you set up structured progress review time to "check and adjust." This is a required element to ensure you maintain a laser focus on achieving your Legacy Goals. This mode fosters an attitude focused on enjoying the journey and a mindset to appreciate obstacles encountered.

Refined by Fire

Obstacles are a signal of progress. **Your biggest growth will often originate from lessons gained during trials and tribulations.** It's when you look at your progress and trajectory and say, *This happened unexpectedly; what can I learn and how do I get back on track?*

You will be refined by fire if you let yourself go through the journey of self-discovery after hardship. Lean in and let go. Some people choose to complain or to play the victim card. While these are both options, my challenge to you is to *get excited*. Embrace the idea of becoming refined by fire and what lies on the other side of adversity.

> *"True intuitive expertise is learned from prolonged experience with good feedback on mistakes."*
>
> —Daniel Kahneman
> author & winner of Nobel Prize in Economics

Your mindset and habits become the fuel to your success and how you view your journey. Don't delegate your worth or mindset to someone else. Don't give it to your boss, don't give it to your spouse, don't delegate it to somebody you think is more qualified than you. This is *your* journey. You own it! Your mindset and your habits are the fuel and gateway to your success.

How do we embrace obstacles and opportunities? How do we know we're on the right path?

Safety Blanket

During college we are given structure and specific instructions on how to achieve academic success. We're given a syllabus and told what the journey should look like, how many tests to anticipate, and what to expect at the end. We are continually informed if we are on track or off track according to academic expectations.

Exiting the structure of formal schooling causes confusion for many people. This new world thrusts people into an unstructured abyss of possibilities and forces them to fend for themselves. **We've been attached to a security blanket of structure.** Everything has been organized perfectly, and we were told what to do and when to do it (which is the central thesis of the Industrial Age school model). We follow the conveyor belt process and blindly trust it will fully prepare us for predictable outcomes on the other side.

*"From our 'modern' education system to the way
that job requisitions are written and filled,
the majority of today's systems are built upon
antiquated 20th century mentalities and economic
imperatives, many of which are falling by the
wayside in the emerging knowledge economy."*

—Nick J. Murphy
speaker & best-selling author

When you enter the real world, many people have this lingering belief everything will magically work out. The unspoken expectation is the journey will be fairly straightforward without difficulty. Unfortunately, traditional school does not prepare students for the responsibility and accountability to own their journey. Without a structure for success, people can be lured by outside influences and distracted by consumerism or materialism. Without a self-regulating process, your brain and your time are filled with pursuits driving the ambition and profits of somebody else.

If you look at your life and say, "I'm not actively pursuing MY goals," then the suggestions in this book should be a good wake-up call to address your priorities and stop being a pawn in someone else's profit.

Set Your Own Syllabus

The first time I truly appreciated the idea of owning my growth track and creating my own syllabus of success was when I committed to unlocking new career opportunities. I wasn't 100% certain of where my career was going. Through the assistance of my mentor, I drafted three versions of my career track which had a high probability of being fulfilling. Two of these versions of the future would benefit from more specialized finance knowledge.

Pursuing an MBA with a finance concentration would give me a holistic overview of managing a business or brand. Feeling behind in my career and believing I could achieve more than just an MBA, I decided on also pursuing the CFA® designation: Chartered Financial Analyst. Achieving this designation requires passing a series of three exams. It just might be the hardest test you've never heard of. Essentially, it's the gold standard in the investment world. It's a rigorous test with three pass/fail levels that is extremely challenging.

I committed to these two programs and began to reverse engineer what the journey would look like. What days were classes? What days could I study? What time of the day could I block out on a regular basis to study? I did this all the way down to the daily numbers of pages that I needed to read to stay on track.

This up-front investment of time allowed me to know if I was pacing correctly during my valleys of uncertainty or periods where I fell behind because of illness or work deliverables. There were certainly weeks and months where I was doubtful, uncertain of how I would complete the MBA course and the CFA® material simultaneously—all while working full-time.

Having a calibration point helped me understand when I was on track for the week, and it gave me a chance to rest and unplug when I reached my weekly progress goals. I could feel good about switching to entertainment-consumption mode, having completed my 80/20 Actions for the week. Another success point was having a vocally supportive wife who stood by me through hard times when I didn't make the best decisions for our relationship.

So what does my feedback loop like today? My biggest time commitments revolve around corporate job and family. Working at Nike pays the bills, but true fulfillment comes from pursuing my purpose of making others better and spending time with my beautiful wife and two amazing kiddos. Leveraging the Legacy Goal framework continues to clarify my vision and gives me more confidence for the future.

By this point, I'm sure you have picked up on the fact that writing this book was a major component of my 6-month goals. It was time to stop passively thinking about writing a book and finally do something about the idea burning inside. At first I didn't know where to start, but I began to seek clarity and focus during my whitespace contemplation time.

After aligning with Lisa, I committed to waking up at 4:30 in the morning. This would allow one hour of writing time each day before a morning workout at 5:30. **Leveraging weekly and daily progress checkpoints has been very energizing psychologically**.

With incremental finish lines, I experience the feeling of success on a regular basis. By the fact that you are reading this book, I've achieved my 6-month goal of publishing a book. I chose my mountain and committed to reaching the top.

Setting up these incremental victories in the short term, these mini finish lines, will give you huge amounts of energy and excitement. The momentum and confidence will allow you to break through doubt when it comes (because it will!). When I doubted my ability to complete the MBA and CFA® course work simultaneously, I went back to my roadmap and looked at my progress to date. After seeing all my past victories, I could not logically conclude quitting was an option because I had already accomplished many short-term victories. That insight gave me the energy to keep running the race to the next mini finish line. These mini-victories became my internal cheerleader, encouraging me to take one more step on the winding road of progress.

Linear Growth Fallacy

Growth is a messy endeavor. Challenging but fun! You will need to embrace the idea of calibration to make sure you remain on track. Think of an airplane traveling from Los Angeles to New York. How often do you think the plane is officially "on track"? The average flight will be off-course 90-95% of the time. Said differently, *the plane is headed precisely the correct direction 5-10% of the time.* Are the pilots freaking out? Nope! They know calibration is part of reaching their destination. Or think of your last car ride. You reached your destination by keeping your eyes focused ahead and hands always calibrating the steering wheel.

Through calibration, you'll be able to make micro-adjustments and remain on course through the entire journey of your life.

What do you think personal growth or progress should look like? Should it be predictable? Are setbacks acceptable? If so, how many setbacks are tolerated before applying the label of "failure"? People tend to give themselves zero leeway for setbacks or missteps as they pursue growth.

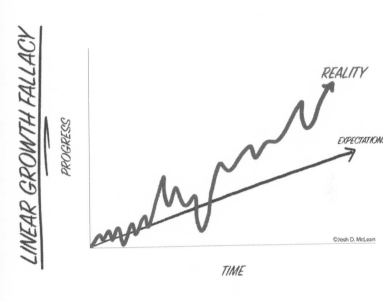

Overcoming an obstacle is something we often celebrate in other people. Somehow we are unwilling to give ourselves the same encouragement. Why is that? I've found something changes when we turn the mirror on ourselves.

I'm here to tell you growth should not be predictable. Each step will not be smooth and predictably higher than the next. This is the **Linear Growth Fallacy** in action. People believe their growth has to be in a upward trajectory 100% of the time or else they have somehow failed.

Personal growth comes from taking risks and embracing a non-linear journey.

Move forward with confidence. You've got this!

IT'S YOUR TURN.

TIME TO TAKE ACTION.

BE AWESOME.

BE BOLD.

BE YOU.

TAKE ACTION :: FEEDBACK LOOP

During this chapter, we've talked about being refined by fire, the safety of structure, setting your own success syllabus, and the Linear Growth Fallacy.

Here is a list of actions to get you moving:

DAILY

Ensure you have regular morning reflection time. Put this in your calendar and make it non-negotiable. This should take no longer than five or ten minutes. I like to put it after my meditation or gratitude time.

Review your 2-week horizon of 80/20 Actions and ask yourself these questions:

> » What actions do I need to take today to move these goals forward?
> » What task do I fear the most?
> » What will give me the most energy?
> » What am I grateful for?
> » Who needs my A-game? (I got this one from Brendon Burchard)

WEEKLY

Leverage weekly reflection time. Make sure this is in your calendar and non-negotiable. I've gotten into the habit of blocking off Sunday nights, spending anywhere from 30 minutes to a couple hours, depending on how much depth is required. If just doing quick a calibration, 30 minutes should be sufficient.

A few questions to consider:

> » Was the week successful?
> » Were my weekly goals achieved? Why or why not?
> » What was my biggest surprise?
> » What gave me the most energy?

Then turn this insight to the upcoming week and ask things like these:

> » For this upcoming week, what is going to make it successful?
> » What do I need to achieve?
> » What's going to give me the most energy?

RELATIONSHIPS

Schedule regular time with your spouse. This is the most important relationship in your life. Get their perspective and prioritize any insights with urgency. If you are not married, make sure to carve out time to connect with meaningful people in your life.

PERSPECTIVE

Schedule regular time with your mentor, or keep in contact with a peer pacing with you on the road to personal transformation. What are they seeing that you might be missing? Can you leverage each other's energy and victories?

BE CURIOUS

BEHIND THE CURTAIN

*"To give anything less than your
best is to sacrifice the gift."*

—Steve "Pre" Prefontaine
rebel & track trailblazer

Why Now?

It might be helpful for me to share why I'm writing
this book now versus exploring other avenues. Why
did I choose to write a book before coaching or before
speaking? Identifying my mission to serve others and
make others better required me to explore impact

opportunities outside of mentoring others within a corporate setting.

Understanding my passion around personal growth and power of my voice helped bring focus to avenues I might use to influence others. Carefully considering my kryptonite I had to strategically neutralize the fear of my voice. The best way to accomplish this was through publishing a book. It will be an important point of validation and a point of strength for me to leverage as start the journey of public speaking. When doubt comes flooding in before my first speech I will have "proof" of my purpose and impact to the world.

Publishing this book officially gets my ideas out into the world with no ability to take it back. I don't anticipate knocking someone off the New York Times bestseller top spot, but I have great confidence it's the best book and the best material I can write. The output of this book is better than any half-written book in my head.

Getting Started

Without the six steps contained within this book I would have not taken the first step of writing. Starting this journey was rife with **psychological warfare** as I was reminded of my past shortcomings at even the thought of writing a book.

In this new pass at writing a book, I had to be aware of my prior pitfalls and create new sparks of action. I hired a coach and set up mental games to get past the research point and actually start writing. Eventually I got to a point where my mind map was fleshed out and my outline was almost complete. However, my coach was there to challenge me and highlight that I was spending too much time on my outline.

Reflecting internally, I was actually afraid to start writing. **I was procrastinating, but on the outside it looked like I was taking action.** Nobody knew except for my coach; he was close to my work and an expert in helping people reach their self-publishing goals. He called me out and said, "Why have you not started writing?" Guilty.

At this point I had to recommit to my goals. I acknowledged the fear but also used my whitespace time to listen for those quiet, subtle hints. During my daily check-in time, it became clear I was avoiding taking all the necessary action. That allowed me to quickly pivot and make micro-calibrations toward successfully publishing my book.

What was holding me back? What do I fear most? Fear of putting my message out in the world was still lingering in my head. What did I need to change? What could I do differently? I heard others talk about dictating their book. I could try that. What's the harm? The idea of dictating the book came into focus but was still a little scary. I'm not currently a podcaster, I don't own a microphone, so the process was somewhat of a mystery.

By vocalizing my intentions, I encountered an expert who helped me simplify the process and take the next action. Every chapter you read in this book started out as a transcription from speaking from my outline into my iPhone. The process of dictating my book suddenly became exciting and much more energizing than the thought of starting from scratch writing on a blank page.

After getting the transcription back from my first recorded chapter, I quickly dictated the second chapter. I sat back and thought "I can do this." I started on a Monday with zero words on paper, just an outline of ideas I wanted to cover. My daily writing target was 1,000 words and my stretch goal was 1,500. That first day I spent about an hour and a half going through this dictation process and ended—in one day—with 5,500 words on paper.

One small decision allowed me to go from a fearful guy with an outline to blowing my stretch target out of the water. This created tremendous momentum in a space that caused apprehension 24 hours earlier.

Anything is possible if you align your
energy and focus against the goal!

**SELF-PUBLISHING
SCHOOL**

NOW IT'S YOUR TURN

Discover the EXACT 3-step blueprint you need to become a bestselling author in 3 months. Self-Publishing School helped me, and now I want them to help you with this FREE WEBINAR!

Even if you're busy, bad at writing, or don't know where to start, you CAN write a bestseller and build your best life.

With tools and experience across a variety of niches and professions, Self-Publishing School is the most efficient resource you need to take your book to the finish line!

DON'T WAIT!

Watch this FREE VIDEO TRAINING SERIES now, and say "YES" to becoming a bestseller:

www.bit.ly/SelfPublishWebinar

READY TO WRITE YOUR OWN BOOK?

Drop me a note
and let me know your topic!

linkedin.com/in/joshmclean

or

Josh@catalystignite.com

ABOUT THE AUTHOR

Josh is a continual learner energized by the pursuit of eliminating overwhelm and helping people achieve their full potential. He resides in Portland, Oregon, with his beautiful wife and two amazing kiddos.

Life is good today but that wasn't always the case. Over the last decade, Josh has overcome the crippling effect of fear as well as a severe car accident that resulted in a brain injury.

His life proves small actions and a strong mindset can spark transformation change.

QUOTE ATTRIBUTIONS

INTRODUCTION

Olson, Jeffrey G. *The Slight Edge: Turning Simple Disciplines into Massive Success.* 8th ed. Lake Dallas, TX: Success Books.

Robinson, Ken. "Bring on the Learning Revolution!" TED: Ideas worth Spreading. 2010. Accessed October 07, 2018. https://www.ted.com/talks/sir_ken_robinson_bring_on_the_revolution/transcript?language=en.

Olson, Jeffrey G. *The Slight Edge: Turning Simple Disciplines into Massive Success.* 8th ed. Lake Dallas, TX: Success Books.

STEP ONE: CREATE MARGIN

"Aristotle." Aristotle - Wikiquote. Accessed October 07, 2018. https://en.wikiquote.org/wiki/Talk:Aristotle.

Levitin, Daniel. "Why It's So Hard To Pay Attention, Explained By Science." Fast Company. September 25, 2015. Accessed October 07, 2018. https://www.fastcompany.com/3051417/why-its-so-hard-to-pay-attention-explained-by-science.

Elrod, Hal. *The Miracle Morning: The Not-So-Obvious Secret Guaranteed to Transform Your Life before 8AM.* Place of Publication Not Identified: Hal Elrod International, 2014.

"Neuroplasticity." Wikipedia. September 21, 2018. Accessed October 07, 2018. https://en.wikipedia.org/wiki/Neuroplasticity.

Robbins, Tony. "Key to Success: 3 Secrets to Turn Your Dreams Into Reality." Tonyrobbins.com. Accessed October 07, 2018. https://www.tonyrobbins.com/stories/unleash-the-power/the-key-to-success-model-the-best/.

Koch, Richard. *The 80/20 Principle: the Secret of Achieving More with Less.* Currency Doubleday, 2008.

STEP TWO: IDENTIFY YOUR SUPERPOWERS

Cain, Susan. *Quiet: The Power of Introverts in a World That Cant Stop Talking.* London: Penguin Books, 2013.

"CliftonStrengths | Gallup." Gallup. Accessed October 07, 2018. https://www.gallupstrengthscenter.com/.

Waitzkin, Josh. *The Art of Learning: An Inner Journey to Optimal Performance.* New York: Free Press, 2008.

Jobs, Steve. "'You've Got to Find What You Love,' Jobs Says." 2005 Commencement Address. June 14, 2005. Accessed October 07, 2018. https://news.stanford.edu/news/2005/june15/jobs-061505.html.

STEP THREE: NEUTRALIZE YOUR KRYPTONITE

"Meditations." Wikipedia. October 04, 2018. Accessed October 07, 2018. https://en.wikipedia.org/wiki/Meditations.

"7 Motivational Quotes to Help You Face Your Fears (Because Worry Never Fixes Anything)." SUCCESS. July 31, 2018. Accessed October 07, 2018. https://www.success.com/7-motivational-quotes-to-help-you-face-your-fears-because-worry-never-fixes-anything/.

Dalio, Ray. *Principles: Life and Work*. Simon and Schuster, 2017.

Slap, Stan. *Bury My Heart at Conference Room B: The Unbeatable Impact of Truly Committed Managers*. London: Portfolio Penguin, 2012.

Bishop, Gary John. *Unf*ck Yourself: Get out of Your Head and into Your Life*. Yellow Kite, 2018.

STEP FOUR: SET LEGACY GOALS

Sincero, Jen. *You Are a Badass*. Philadelphia: Running Press, 2017.

Official Site of Coach Wooden. Accessed October 07, 2018. http://www.coachwooden.com/.

"Will Smith Quotes (Author of *Just the Two of Us*)." Goodreads. Accessed October 07, 2018. https://www.goodreads.com/author/quotes/598671.Will_Smith.

"Famous Pablo Picasso Quotes." The Weeping Woman, 1937 by Pablo Picasso. Accessed October 07, 2018. https://www.pablopicasso.org/quotes.jsp.

Dalio, Ray. *Principles: Life and Work*. Simon and Schuster, 2017.

Fried, Jason, and David Heinemeier. Hansson. *Rework*. London: Vermilion, 2010.

STEP FIVE: CREATE SUCCESS SPARKS

"Anthony Robbins." Anthony Robbins - Wikiquote. Accessed October 07, 2018. https://en.wikiquote.org/wiki/Anthony_Robbins.

"Newton's Laws of Motion." Wikipedia. October 06, 2018. Accessed October 07, 2018. https://en.wikipedia.org/wiki/Newton's_laws_of_motion.

"In January Guideposts: Denzel Washington Talks about Mentoring and Who His Role Models Were." Business Wire. December 27, 2006. Accessed October 07, 2018. https://www.businesswire.com/news/home/20061227005002/en/January-Guideposts-Denzel-Washington-Talks-Mentoring-Role.

STEP SIX: FEEDBACK LOOP

"Open Your World, Walk Towards Wisdom - An Interview with Dr. Ken Blanchard." Steve Kayser. October 05, 2018. Accessed October 07, 2018. http://stevekayser.com/open-your-world-walk-towards-wisdom-interview-with-best-selling-author-dr-ken-blanchard/.

Kahneman, Daniel. "Don't Blink! The Hazards of Confidence." The New York Times. October 19, 2011. Accessed October 07, 2018. https://www.nytimes.com/2011/10/23/magazine/dont-blink-the-hazards-of-confidence.html.

Murphy, Nick J. "Education System Flaws." E-mail message to author. September 2018.

"Programs." CFA Institute. Accessed October 07, 2018. http://www.cfainstitute.org/programs.

BEHIND THE CURTAIN

"40 Years of Prefontaine." Nike News. Accessed October 07, 2018. https://news.nike.com/news/40-years-of-prefontaine.

Made in the USA
Middletown, DE
15 February 2021

33798415R10113